Living
in
Love

Also by Alexandra Stoddard

WILLIAM MORROW AND COMPANY, INC.

New York

Alexandra Stoddard

Living *in* Love

It is the policy of William Morrow and Company, Inc.,
and its imprints and affiliates, recognizing the importance of preserving what has been written, to print the
books we publish on acid-free paper, and we exert our
best efforts to that end.

Library of Congress Cataloging-in-Publication Data
Stoddard, Alexandra.
    Living in love / Alexandra Stoddard.
      p.   cm.
    ISBN 0-688-14338-5
    1. Love.   2. Stoddard, Alexandra.   I. Title.
BF575.L8S825   1997
306.7—dc20   96-35369
                                                  CIP

Printed in the United States of America

First Edition

1 2 3 4 5 6 7 8 9 10

BOOK DESIGN BY MARYSARAH QUINN

To Peter

Contents

Living
in
Love

1.

"There Will Be a Lot of Surprises."

Here is someone at once so like you that you have come home, and yet so different he opens a thousand windows on the universe.

— MICHAEL DRURY

Dear Peter,

I believe my eternal commitment to you began when we first met in 1954. Now I experience all love through the prism of ours. We all have access to the boundless energy force that is love. When we tap into this divine gift, you are me and I am you. We complete each other. What's missing in my life, you make up for. I'm whole because of you. I love you completely and love you just as you are because you bring me variety and fresh ideas; you stimulate me, and I am inspired by your energy. Your fertile imagination helps me maintain a youthful spirit. Just as dancing replenishes psychic energy, the more loving I become, the more lovable I am. And I adore being loved by you. My heart skips a beat when I think of you, and sometimes when I go for a walk I end up skipping. Your active mind and gentle decorum bring me lyrical joy and often oceanic feelings where I continuously rediscover myself.

The love I feel for life is the flame in my heart. Whenever I aim my energy in the direction of loving you, I am loving the spark inside me and I'm all keyed up with pleasure. Our meeting place is love and life itself is the aphrodisiac. There is no magic to keeping our love alive, no better aphrodisiac than our loving energy. Aphrodisiac comes from Aphrodite, the Greek goddess of love and beauty. Love of family, love of friends, love of art, love of music, love of learning are all aphrodisiacs. A piece of Godiva chocolate is an aphrodisiac. An oval bar of pure white almond soap is an aphrodisiac. Your tenderness toward your children is an aphrodisiac. Your love of nature is an aphrodisiac. The love of color is an aphrodisiac. A beautiful day is an aphrodisiac. Your marvelous sense of humor is an aphrodisiac. We can arouse and intensify all our desires when we're loving and focusing on what is beautiful. The more we love life the more radiant and lovable we become. You are alive in my consciousness and I can actually feel my invisible, nonphysical loving energy day and night, whenever I am still, and able to connect to my nobler self.

If I ever let you down, in whatever ways, I will first be letting myself down. I have an unquestionable belief in our ability to laser-focus our sensibilities and innate talents for living in love and releasing our full potency. If we have an emotional excess, let it be tilted toward love. I have an inescapable urge to connect the eons of time and space that separate us and bring us together with clarity and a charitable heart. I'd love to ease a burden, wipe away a tear and, through the pure energy of love, be a part of your life, merging beatitudes, where we are vehicles of love, communicating grace, awakening natural joys in you, and opening up supernatural powers of celestial reverie, quenching your thirst when you need love. Our flesh and soul are one, and your laughing eyes and smile are sacred. We're carrying so much love we're able to conjure up a paradise right here.

And because we are solid in an abundance of love and mutual support, we're both free to love the world and all those loving people we know and meet from around the globe on this amazingly wondrous adventure. I entrust my life to love, believing in its powerful gift of grace and capacity for joy. All we have to do is trust life and try not to interfere.

Our consciousness of love is ageless, gender free, and eternal. Everything I have ever loved fuels the fire of passion and heats the pure blood flowing through my veins. I'm lifted up and swept away into a place that is sweet-smelling, pure, and intoxicating. I'm reminded of sucking honeysuckle as a child, or making grape jelly after picking the plumpest, juiciest grapes from the arbor. I'm united with a host of loving people.

We live in chapters, as best we can, trying to learn from our divine nature. Only in our soulful, tranquil moments can we sort through the noise and confusion of current events and move into a timeless perspective, where we're able to interpret a bigger view of truth, in the quiescence of our private sanctuary. No one judges us harshly as we sort out our own needs and those of others, figuring out what to do, who to love and what to hope for, adjusting to the changing conditions of life, and seeking to alter favorably our patterns and conditioning so we become less shortsighted, less self-destructive, less apathetic, dogmatic, and limiting.

In these times of reflection, I want to become more inquisitive, less self-righteous, more tolerant. Privately, quietly, we refract prejudices, breaking up and deflecting from a straight path as the bending of light waves when they pass from one medium into another. Here, I don't want to hold myself back, to feel restrained in my thinking, but allow myself to enter into the more generous, giving aspects of my nature. Quietly I want to use my ingenuity to direct and redirect my energies so I can recharge my spirit, becoming more energetic, curious, vivacious, and creative.

When we come together in complete privacy, we anticipate a dependability that becomes part of the indelible imprint these moments leave on us. The worrisome edginess of "out there" gives way to visceral feelings that metaphorically connect us in our imaginings with nuances of our soul. How we feel testifies to the ineffable spirit of love.

Life is ephemeral, fleeting. But in our short time on earth we have enough time to live in love, growing in grace and empathy. I've felt over the years a wide range of emotions, as we all have, and my growing realization that we can beam our own heart and soul toward greater love becomes stronger every day. We are all, I am now convinced, generously endowed with potentiality for happiness. This is the story, *our* story, I want to tell.

Love,

Alexandra

Surprised by Love

On the afternoon Peter and I decided to join our lives together, we stood in front of a warm fire holding each other tightly. I can't remember whether our hug lasted for a few seconds or all afternoon. Whatever its duration, it was the beginning of a lifetime of living in love. That afternoon, Peter kissed my lips and looked at me with a grin reserved only for me and said, "There will be a lot of surprises." I couldn't imagine what surprises he was referring to; I didn't give it a thought. We'd be together, we'd work things out. All that mattered at that moment was the joy we were feeling because of our commitment.

Love is the sensory and emotional experience of union. Boundaries are dissolved in love and we form unities with people, places, and things.

—Jay B. Rohrlich

As it turns out, living in love with Peter has indeed been full of surprises of every conceivable kind, starting with our unlikely decision to get married, orchestrated by my daughter Brooke, a four-year-old. Deciding to marry Peter was both an easy and an impossible choice to make. We had been good friends for more than twenty years. We had known each other and stayed in touch ever since his sister Bebe introduced us outside the tennis court where we had just finished a ladies' doubles match. After the end of Peter's second marriage and the breakup of my first marriage, we became a great source of comfort and pleasure for each other. We were good friends, but never anything more. One day, while Peter was playing with Brooke, who was enchanted by his company, she turned to him, threw her arms around his neck, and proposed, "Peter Rabbit, why don't you come live with us?" "I'll have to ask your mother first," Peter said, surprising himself.

That Love is all there is, / Is all we know of Love.

—Emily Dickinson

I had never expected Peter's and my long friendship to be anything but a great companionship. We spent a lot of time with the children, always having so much fun when we were all together, whether we were having a picnic, bike riding, eating out at a restaurant, or dining at my apartment. But Peter was such a wonderful man, a true lover of life, with a generous and energetic spirit. He is sweet to people, and in return people tend to be kind and loving to him. He is also an extraordinarily open man who can express his vulnerability, share his thoughts, and be hugely supportive of those he loves. He believed in me, always encouraging me as both a mother and a professional designer. I felt lucky to know him. He was a great friend, but marriage seemed quite unlikely.

Love is a wealth of community where mind, body, and spirit meet and dissolve, to gather again in new dimensions and forms.

—Michael Drury

I knew that the decision to say yes to Peter would change my life dramatically and permanently, for so many reasons. I was still a little reluctant to marry again. I'd had a mad crush on my first husband, who was my mixed doubles tennis partner. I was captain of the junior New England tennis team and was full of myself and admiration for this guitar-playing, calypso-singing Yale graduate with a lively sense of humor. We were married at a young age: I was nineteen and he was twenty-four. I had a naive fantasy about marriage, and was energized and impassioned by the prospect of having fun all the time. I knew more about my husband's tennis strokes than about what was in his heart and mind, and I was more self-conscious about how I looked going down the aisle than I was about our wedding vows.

Getting married when you are nineteen makes no sense to me now, but in my generation many of us didn't know much about a lot of things. Though I loved him as much as I could love any man at that time in my life, I wasn't prepared for the seriousness and often intense reality of sharing my life with another human being. I still didn't know a lot about myself and I was restless and pre-occupied with finding out. The profound responsibility of caring for another adult with his own mental, emotional, and spiritual needs was daunting. I knew I could make ample room inside my own life for someone else, but first I needed to know more about my *self.*

Give all to love;
Obey the heart;
Friends, kindred, days,
Estate, good fame,
Plans, credit and the
Muse,
Nothing refuse.

—Emerson

By the time Peter and I were contemplating marriage, I was finally comfortable being a single mother of two wonderful daughters, Alexandra and Brooke. I liked the freedom being single gave me to spend all my time with the girls when I wasn't at work, and I was trying to publish my first book. But I missed the companionship of a loving man. I tried to date but that didn't work. I wanted a family, but my relationship with my daughters was so rich and fulfilling, I certainly wasn't looking for any changes that might disturb the balance we'd found at last. I knew that living well with another person required a lot of attention and adjustment.

My relationship with Peter was further complicated by the fact that Peter was fifty-two and I was nineteen years his junior. The significant gap in our ages was a tricky issue: different generations, different friends, and less common ground. I was young and, I was told, attractive, and many people suspected that I wanted someone to take care of me, even though I was determined to remain independent financially and continue my career in interior design. Women of Peter's generation normally didn't work, so there was no precedent. But none of this really concerned me; the real complications revolved around entering into a situation where there was so much family history—most important, children I hadn't raised.

> *I am a part of all that I have met.*
>
> —*Alfred, Lord Tennyson*

Peter had been married twice and was blessed with six children; all mean a great deal to him. This meant I would have to find a central place in my life not only for Peter, but for his family as well. The children would have their own resistance to our union. This was a situation where no mothers were present to care for Peter's children, who would be part of our new household after we married. Peter, at this stage, was the father and the mother of six children. I felt, despite his love and respect for me, he was reluctant to enter into another marriage where he would be living with two additional children, Alexandra and Brooke, who were six and four.

There was a great deal of disapproval about our decision to marry. My mother, other family members, and friends were outspoken and judgmental. Confronting those who expressed reservations was one of the most difficult challenges of my life. But by trusting my instincts, risking losing the support of family and the confidence of our more conventional friends, I opened the door to a world of love I never knew existed. Deep inside, I knew Peter and I would live in love together. Once we committed ourselves to each other, I no longer sought anyone's approval. The challenge facing us ultimately strengthened our bond, making us more aware of how much we loved each other and wanted to share our lives.

The past is set, the present is now, and the future is unpredictable. Neither of us knew, we agreed, what we were getting into. But we did know we'd established a strong love over the years. Reality and fantasy often differ, a lesson we had both learned through personal experience. We knew we would face obstacles, but there was something that ultimately felt so right about our decision to marry. In the months before our marriage, we revealed more and more about ourselves to each other, losing track of time while talking about our hopes, our fears, and our dreams. We discovered how much we had in common: our love of children, books, and adventure, including travel, architecture, food, design, and art. We also learned about each other's needs, the most significant being our mutual desire to continue to evolve as separate, unique individuals while we also grew as a couple. Neither of us could risk

The first step to take is to become aware that love is an art, just as living is an art; *if we want to learn how to love we must proceed in the same way we have to proceed if we want to learn any other art, say music, painting, carpentry, or the art of medicine or engineering.*

—*Erich Fromm*

being with someone who would inhibit our personal growth and aspirations; we each needed to be with a person who believed in us. We found strength in our openness, in our vulnerability, and in our willingness to face the challenges. We would have to be strong for each other, faithful and committed.

The times we spent together prior to our wedding day, planning and discussing the life we would build together by fusing our independence, flowing into interdependence, were momentous. Peter was fascinated by my energy, my enthusiasm, and my sheer determination to construct a life together rich with meaning. In these months of self-disclosure, when I exposed my essence to Peter unselfconsciously, an awakening of our potential power as a couple emerged. We could see our ability to privately live our lives together following our own path, without fear of criticism from others. Peter and I were deeply attached and compatible in our values, even if not in our experiences. We were ready and ripe, not wanting to waste motion going against the current of our best mutual interests.

Love is real, positive, and a certainty, an affirmation in our orientation toward life.

In those intimate conversations, I felt comfortable expressing my deepest thoughts, trusting Peter not only to listen and understand, but to really pay attention, not holding back for fear of having my dreams seem selfish or unobtainable. By opening myself up to Peter in this way, and he to me, we discovered a strong sense of mutuality, an indication that our separate dreams would remain alive, but now we would pursue them *together.*

Our private times together when we listened to personal stories, encouraging each other to dream extravagantly, counterbalanced the concrete reality of a patchwork family. While domestic negotiations and wedding plans dominate some engaged couples' time alone, we preferred to discuss ideas. Between us, this was our fifth marriage. We knew our focus should not be aimed at the wedding day but on how we could commit ourselves to each other permanently.

We agreed we'd have a small, modest, intimate family wedding in a tiny chapel, in order not to have pageantry cloud over the deeper values we'd need to draw on in our years together. Our secret talks strength-

> *To love deeply in one direction makes us more loving in all others.*
>
> —*Madame Swetchine*

ened our knowledge and understanding of what joys lay ahead. We embraced this union optimistically because we were expe-riencing such exhilaration as we confessed our secret desires, enjoying the privacy of being able to expose our vulnerability in sweet, tender gestures.

A legal document filed away in a drawer doesn't change fun-damental attitudes or patterns. What you see in the months before a marriage is a good indication of what to expect later on. As Peter and I exposed ourselves to each other, our vul-nerability became our strength because we were forming the bedrock of a sound union of souls. Here we were, at the apex of forming a lifelong union with each other. Everything was new.

> *Hello, young lovers, wherever you are.*
>
> —*Oscar Hammerstein*

We had established so much together before the actual mar-riage ceremony, reception, and honeymoon. Our closeness became ingrained in our consciousness. We established a pat-tern during our courtship that we thankfully have maintained.

The two intertwined gold ropes of my wedding ring were a symbolic affirmation of our determination to weave our lives together as gracefully and as beautifully as we could.

Once we decided to live in love together, Peter gave me a hand-hammered necklace of interlocking circles. He put it around my neck and closed the clasp. "Alexandra, darling, this is the continuity of the circle of love, forever. I love you." I want to go to my grave wearing this necklace; I wear it every day. I'm often asked about the significance of this piece of jewelry. I wink and answer, "There's a circle for every year of my life." But because I always wear it, no one knows for sure how old I was when I received this sentimental gift.

The Secret Is Loving Energy

At dinner one evening, recently, our daughter Brooke spoke of the challenges of living: "You have to be prepared for what life has to offer." When I was thirty-three and married Peter, I knew a great deal more about myself and was by then prepared and mature enough to make a permanent love commitment to another person. This was the most important decision of my life.

I'm going to be speaking about the man I love.

—*Elizabeth Dole*

Our commitment to each other strongly affects the course of our life, and our mutual love of life, because our devotion to each other is profound. We treat one another with affection, cherishing each moment we're blessed to share in love.

In the period when I was a single mother, the world of

living in love was emphasized to me, because I felt free to be and express myself as a unique person without being in the role of wife in a society that had gender expectations. I burst into *being* and discovered how liberating it was for me to be myself. It was not my husband who had restricted my freedom, but the position of "Mrs." when I was still emotionally a "Miss." Raising and caring for Alexandra and Brooke showed me how much loving energy I was capable of pro-

> *In life there are meetings which seem like fate.*
>
> —*Owen Meredith*

viding without having to play the role of traditional wife. As I wrote in *The Art of the Possible*, "Love is not a constant; it is energy, intention, and action." The enormous discipline, commitment, and effort we put into our own lives brings love back to us one hundredfold. Loving energy generates love, but first we must feel centered and free to *be* and *become* who we truly are meant to be.

The Commitment to Love

Our circumstances will always provide challenges, whether there is a significant age difference, stepchildren, different faith, family, health, or money problems, or recovering from abandonment or abuse. It's up to us to build a foundation for love from our own inner resources, disciplining ourselves to function productively, being positive in our thoughts and actions. The potential to live in love is always inside us, and it's up to us to release this inner essence without blocking the divine flow. Love, I've come to know, is the central element of our lives; nothing else can ever substitute for this belief. The crowning glory of our life is to be a loving person.

"Lasting love is something a person has to decide to experience," wrote Robert Wright in *The Moral Animal*. When we are capable of making this decision, all our energy is directed toward building love in every aspect of our daily lives.

> *Each person's smile at a particular moment constitutes a unique event in the history of mankind.*
>
> —*René Dubos*

Love requires gratitude, forgiveness, commitment, and faith, to an awesome degree. When we come together we must do so with compassion and dignity, making it our solemn promise to protect each other and be there together, regardless of the challenges. Our faith will be tested. We know how difficult it often is to maintain our own inner peace. Love, as with all important things in life, requires us to always go the extra mile, to rise to a higher self, to find strength, courage, and reason where there seems to be little, to move deliberately toward understanding when we feel uncertain, and to have faith in our true selves no matter what we're forced to confront. How we act and react is in our control, not the outside events that affect us. By our commitment to being a loving person, moment to moment, we rise to living in love.

> *We do not know where we are going but we are on our way.*
>
> —*Stephen Vincent Benét*

I somehow understood this sense of oneness with myself when I was three years old in my mother's flower garden. I learned early in life that without the foundation of dedication and passion, nothing important can follow. Within four years of this awareness I happily became a gardener. I worked hard in my garden, and through this intense labor of love I learned that seeds can flourish under proper cultivation. I could not articulate my feelings, but in that moment of mystical joy, I felt such bliss, and I now know from experience that what I was feeling was love. I always try to do whatever is necessary to rise above life's setbacks and to meet challenging situations head on. I continue to find ways to cope and even, if lucky, to thrive, regardless of circumstances.

There is nothing holier, in this life of ours, than the first consciousness of love—the first fluttering of its silken wings.

—Henry Wadsworth Longfellow

When we commit to another in marriage, we make this pledge of devotion, formally promising to act lovingly. Our vows to each other are a sacred commitment to support each other's total being, each other's spiritual, intellectual, emotional, and creative growth. We bind our higher self to another higher self, unifying our moral integrity with one another. Love is an energy, not a fancy conceit, but a divine force inside us. We must train ourselves to stay as balanced as a canoe in this love consciousness because this is our true nature. Love comes from giving energy flowing out from us into those we love—invisibly, as grace.

Love awakens us fully.

Love is an absence of narcissism, requiring objectivity and reason laced with humility. When we learn to be humble we paradoxically open up to our innate glory. When we understand the importance of this expansiveness, we have begun to grasp the kind of energy—not the external circumstances—that supports a lifelong commitment to living in love. If someone is angry, hostile, rude, or mean spirited, we must not react in unloving ways. That person is somehow suffering, and our loving energy can help them to heal.

Training to Live in Love

Love requires embracing the world with a fresh consciousness every moment. Each experience, no matter how minor, can be a building block of our whole self, an opportunity to grow, to *feel* life more completely. Self-realization, dignity, and integrity are innate privileges of human beings. All of us know pain and troubles, and have to learn to be courageous so that we can transcend our past and reach a deeper, higher awareness. Over these years I've had increasing faith that we are generously endowed with the potential for growth of our positive productive powers, and can find great happiness in our ability to live in love and in turn produce loving energy in others.

The supreme happiness in life is the conviction that we are loved.

— Victor Hugo

We all have hidden potentialities. To live in love is to realize our possibilities, using *our* potency to go forth and ascend to a more sensitive, kinder, more tender consciousness as a result of the expression of our own productive loving powers. Each of us is capable of growing in and renewing our ability to give love if we care enough about our own life to use our talents well.

*Drink to me only with thine eyes,
And I will pledge with mine.*

—Ben Jonson

Loving energy requires a conscious purpose, practice, and maturity. Being loving also requires preparation, skill, training, and understanding. Peter and I knew this well. For my engagement ring, he changed the words on his family crest from "learn to die" to "learn to love."

When we were children, we were totally dependent on the unconditional love of our mother. We were cared for by others. As mature adults, we have to make a commitment to our self to learn, stand on our own two feet, develop our total personality, and move toward achievement of a positive, productive life. By our attitude and will, we can rise to all occasions, adjusting to situations so we're capable of being noble and whole.

We sought each other long before we met. . . . We found ourselves so mutually taken with one another, so acquainted and so endeared betwixt ourselves, that from thence forward nothing was ever so near to us as one another. . . . Being begun so late, there was no time to lose.

—*Michel de Montaigne*

There is a conflicting expectation among immature lovers who haven't experienced enough of life's realities. They believe life should be all smooth sailing. It never is. We understand love within the organization of living. Knowledge is freedom, liberating us from negative fears. The synthesis of our total being is what we're summoned to seek. Our quest for fresh union is our capacity to release love from within, connecting, being attached to life's positive forces. We are no longer alone or lonely because we are united in this mystical, mysterious way.

Love needs attention and thoughtful nurturing. I can't neglect a child and love that child. I can't neglect my self and love my self. I can't neglect my writing and love to write. I can't neglect my home and still love our house. With a loving attitude and outlook, all we ever loved and love now is fused in all reality—in people, places, and things.

The pleasure of love is in loving.

—*La Rochefoucauld*

There is a direct correlation between universal love and individuality. I am one and you are one but together we are also one. In order to love on a higher spiritual beam, we have to love how our souls are connected in this broad perspective. We learn to be more loving in every aspect of our lives, to become more sensitive, caring people, capable of reaching higher powers of mind and spirit. When we come to know that another person *is* us, we are intuitively more sympathetic to their feelings because we know our own.

To live in this attitude and energy of love we should continue to "be there" for each other, always in spirit if we cannot be together physically. If we each have faith in the mystery of love, no matter what happens in our earthly life together, we'll be strong because we've made a leap of faith—in life and love. Our highest devotion is to each other. We live with this inner knowledge and experience it each day and this eternal love is our way to transcend death.

The essence of relationship is that in the encounter both persons are changed.

—*Rollo May*

Peter and I never fell in love, we grew in love gradually, as friends, and we are still growing. When you fall, you hurt yourself, and too many people start off well together, only to have the relationship fall apart over time. After an initial physical, chemical combustion, over time the attraction may fizzle, and the relationship may deteriorate into division of domestic labor.

Friendship, someone once wrote, is the marriage of the soul. Peter and I have become soul mates. In the process of caring for ourselves, our children, and each other, we grow more affectionate and deeper in love. I never knew I was capable of loving one man this deeply. I wasn't fully prepared to live in love to this degree of intensity over so many years. But because each of us is able to continue to evolve individually while our relationship expands, we are continuously learning what it takes to help love grow. My greatest surprise in life is how empowered by love Peter and I continue to be. To our amazement, Peter and I have found more enlightenment, more happiness together, than either of us ever thought possible.

The micro-moment of awareness that my eye truly meets your eye . . . is the moment of Truth, of the Fullness of Life, beyond love, beyond friendship.

—*Frederick Frank*

It is safe to say, looking back, I had a love of life that was my essential nature when Peter and I decided to marry. In his quintessential book on love, *The Art of Loving*, Erich Fromm put in words what I instinctively knew and has been confirmed over and over in my life with Peter:

Love gives me energy.

—*Peter Megargee Brown*

> Love is not a relationship to a specific person; it is an attitude, an ordination of character which determines the relatedness of the person to the world as a whole, not toward one object of love. If a person loves only one other person and is indifferent to the rest of his fellow men, his love is not love but a symbiotic attachment or an enlarged egotism.

Every loving experience I've had throughout my life brings more loving energy, a more loving attitude to my relationships to other people. If you have genuine self-respect, chances are in favor of you respecting me and treating me with dignity. If your life is well integrated, chances are you will treat me in a balanced, appropriate manner. We are not born with all the expertise we need in the art of loving because we need a whole lot of living in love to hone our skills. The Israeli philosopher Martin Buber speaks not of you and me but the space between us. I consider the space between another human soul and me sacred, because the love that fills this space is genuine, beautiful, truthful, kind, and graceful.

Peter and I continue to enjoy hours of tenderness, both in our conversations as well as in our loving. When we begin to understand love as an attitude, we realize we are not two spirits becoming one spirit, but we become one with the universal loving energy.

2.

Love
Begins
with You

*Every circumstance and
situation gives you the
opportunity to choose this path,
to allow your soul to shine
through you, to bring into the
physical world through you its
unending and unfathomable
reverence for and love of life.*

— GARY ZUKAV

Being Loving to Ourselves

Love is a wondrous miracle. It has power to heal. Love can overcome pain. Love can transform our struggles into opportunities for joy and a deeper appreciation for life.

The first step we take on our miraculous journey toward greater love is to open up the wellspring of love within ourselves. Everything we could ever hope for, intimacy, friendship, and connectedness to life, begins when we draw upon the love that exists within us. Loving anyone or anything is only possible when we know how it feels to have loving feelings, and only when we love ourselves can we be generous, giving love to others. As Olga Butterworth, the spiritual partner and wife of Eric Butterworth, leader of New York's Unity Center, tells us, "We need to walk through life with an open hand, not a clenched fist."

No one can say "I love you" who feels as a nobody. You have to regain yourself before you can give yourself away.

— Theodor Reik

But are we loving enough to love ourselves? Can we give ourselves the support and compassion we so freely give to others? The Old Testament tells us to "love thy neighbor as thyself." Paul Tillich, in a review of Erich Fromm's book *The Sane Society,* stated his preference for the terms "natural self-affirmation" and "paradoxical self-acceptance" to Fromm's "self-love" that he felt was too ambiguous in describing the embracing of one's self in love.

The paradox is that the measure of love we're capable of giving to others comes from our innate feelings of self-worth, how much we value life, as well as what our vision of love is. Only when we nurture our *self*, doing whatever it takes to feel inner peace and compassion toward ourselves, are we free to be loving toward others.

My closest relation is myself.

— Terence

There is no way we can please everyone, a lesson I learned as a little girl when I preferred gardening and climbing trees to playing with dolls. I understand that I will inevitably let others down in certain situations, but I know if I let myself down the results are far more harmful. As I was getting up from my chair to give a talk in Denver, a woman said to me "Don't let me down, Alexandra." I told her afterward, "Anita, I try not to let myself down." When you realize you cannot be all things to all people, you don't have to feel guilty when others are off their path. When you are allowed to do what seems and feels right to you, your love will radiate from inside you, outwardly toward others. When we try to please others at the expense of being true to ourselves, we will always fail and suffer negative consequences.

When you realize the divine Self within you, you are launched beyond superficial living like a missile.

—Bhagavadgita

When we have difficulty loving ourselves, we risk feeling unlovable, unworthy, and undesirable. Rather than opening our hearts, we tighten up and become critical of ourselves. But what would we do if our child, spouse, or a friend confessed to these bad feelings about themselves? Surely we would try to ease their suffering. Wouldn't we comfort them by reminding them how much we love them; how much they mean to us? We'd likely let them know that we understand their pain. Maybe we'd offer to take them out for dinner or for ice cream. Maybe we'd take them for a long walk, or perhaps we'd watch a funny movie together. Maybe we'd hold them as they cried and kiss away their tears.

Now ask yourself: Would you offer the same loving care and kindness to yourself? Surprisingly, many do not. But when we're able to be a source of love to ourselves through the inevitable rough patches, accepting that we are not in control of the weather nor of other people's ability to love, we grow in love not only for ourselves, but for others and for life. Love becomes our nature, radiating from inside us as an energy and attitude. All love flows along the same current; we love ourselves, life, people, and objects from the same divine source.

The overwhelming blessing of love is not another person but oneself, a sudden seeing, a coming into one's own fullness and capacity.

—*Michael Drury*

Maintaining a sense of balance and delight in life depends on our ability to be as kind to ourselves as we want others to treat us. What kind of love I want from you I must first give myself. If this loving energy exists in the space between us, we both grow in self-affirmation and self-acceptance. There is no need to become overwhelmed by sad feelings. If someone habitually feels sorrowful and unhappy, this unnatural state causes weariness and gloom in others. Other people's destructive behavior, tragic circumstances, mistakes, and disappointment at work or in love are part of everyone's life. There are many times when we cannot be on top of the world, but our own private world can remain loving. We can use difficult times as opportunities to exercise our loving skills, to be self-nurturing rather than self-critical.

When my older brother Powell died during open heart surgery, I was able to be a loving presence for his wife and children. Self-love requires the same respect, confidence, commitment, tenderness, courage, attentiveness, generosity, strength of character, and enthusiasm as it does to love others. Love is willing our lives toward light, truth, goodness, and beauty; it is a commitment, a promise to our higher selves.

> *You have to find yourself first and everything else follows.*
>
> —*Lin Yutang*

Is it possible, I wonder, for human beings to love others and not their *selves*? How contradictory it would be to attempt to be a constant source of love to others and an empty well to ourselves. When we understand that our *self* is our total being, our individuality and personality, knowing how to sustain feelings of self-love is the key to a healthy, productive life. Our lives will be suffused with love whenever we remain true to ourselves. The soil where we nurture love is this self, this unique spirit. We don't love when it's convenient or only when we're with others. Love is not a light switch to be turned on and off as circumstances dictate. Only when I remain open and feel loving toward myself can I send genuine loving energy in the direction of others.

> *To a loving person, everybody is worthy of love, every occasion is an opportunity to practice love.*
>
> —*Eknath Easwaran*

If someone is unloving, it is usually because their loving meridians have been blocked by illness, depression, or hostility. In these circumstances, we must always keep in our mind and hearts that we are in charge of our will, including the way we treat ourselves and others. We are the author of our self, and we have the ability to rekindle love within ourselves and a positive attitude toward life and others. Marcus Aurelius, the wise Roman emperor said, "Such as are thy habitual thoughts, such also will be the character of the mind, for the soul is dyed by the thoughts."

Last year I was in an elevator going up to my daughter Brooke's office. The day was excitingly beautiful. I smiled at a pretty young woman. "What a glorious day," I said to her. "Yeah," she answered in a dull tone, "Too bad it won't last." But the glass can always be half full, not half empty. Powell paid me a sweet compliment when I was ten. "Sandie, you like it all. When it's sunny you go out to play and when it rains you're glad you don't have to water or weed your garden."

> *The heart is like a garden. It can grow compassion or fear, resentment, or love. What seeds will you plant there?*
>
> *—Buddha*

I've had my share of difficult times, agonizingly painful moments, some of earthshaking horror. My younger brother Chip, who took his own life, was the best-looking of his siblings and the smartest. He was also the most sensitive. But ever since an LSD episode while serving in the Vietnam War he had not been himself, and life had become a living hell for him. As much as I wanted to help Chip, I could not save him from himself. We learn in life that we cannot be everyone's savior, rescuing the world from all harm, danger, and loss. Chip spent the remaining years of his life in and out of mental institutions, on and off medication, never regaining his *self*. When I visited him in the mental institution, I would always try to bring light into this sorrowful environment, wearing bright clothes and showing a cheerful spirit, but nothing I did or said could break the potent sadness of this place.

When Chip committed suicide, my brother Powell called from Chicago to tell me. Peter and I immediately drove to New Haven to the hospital where they had brought Chip. When we arrived, the head nurse asked, "Are you strong? This will not be easy for you, Mrs. Stoddard. You will not recognize your brother." As I took a deep breath, I felt as though a tennis ball were obstructing my ability to swallow. I nodded affirmatively, "I am now. Thank you." I felt empathy, compassion, and love toward my brother, and at his bedside I tried to convey this affection and concern even though he was brain dead. All my thoughts were on loving him, not on how sad I felt or how sorry I felt for myself. Self-pity is a dangerous thing; the more self-pity you feel, the deeper you sink into the pit of depression. It's a terrible malady, and if it persists it can become near impossible to "snap out of it" and redirect your sight toward a loving consciousness.

He who knows others is wise; He who knows himself is enlightened.

—*Lao-tzu*

If you would be loved, love and be lovable.

—*Benjamin Franklin*

"Selfishness and self-love, far from being identical, are actually opposites," Erich Fromm taught us. "The selfish person does not love himself too much but too little; in fact he hates himself." Loving ourselves and loving others are one and the same, inseparable.

Is it possible to be generous-spirited toward others while being stingy with ourselves? It is only when we can feel love and compassion for ourselves that we are truly ready to give love from our essence. Offer yourself encouragement. Accept this love that is yours to give yourself. Focus on what is possible for you to do to cultivate a generous spirit toward yourself, and you will surely learn more about what love means. When you live in love you never exclude yourself from the gift of loving kindness, gentleness, and compassion. Love always generates more love because it is energy, and the more vital the power, the more love radiates. Love, when understood, is as powerful as the sun.

Be Yourself

When Peter and I first married, out of respect for him I tried to be the wife I thought I should be, at his side, smiling, at cocktail parties, a doting wife. I mistakenly thought I should look his age and mirror his professional demeanor, and not my own. I wore dowdy, conservative, dreary long dresses, trying to fit into solemn legal ceremonies and courtroom seriousness. I believed that I should be the wife Peter's friends expected of him, someone who worked full time to support him in his career rather than having passionate interests of my own. But I was, and am, a woman who wears chromatically intense colors, short skirts, wild fuchsia and chartreuse tights, who skips and runs rather than stands around.

Life teaches us to be less severe with ourselves and others.

—Johann Wolfgang von Goethe

Even though I was never inhibited when I was alone with Peter, the generation gap between us caused me to try to fit into a society that I hadn't grown into gradually but was thrust into. But I wasn't comfortable in anyone else's clothes. Thankfully, Alexandra and Brooke saved me, helping me de-thug my closet, discarding all the new "fuddy-duddy" clothes that the church thrift shop was happy to receive. I was back to my saturated, happy colors and self.

It was never Peter who made me feel I should look more mature. It was my defensive reaction to seemingly everyone's making such an issue of his maturity and my youth. I even began to walk more slowly until I realized how young Peter was inside. I always sensed that he loved me the way I was. His intention was never to make me over to fit some special image of a wife. He often said, "Never change a thing." He wanted me to be completely myself. One of the greatest attractions, from the first time we met, has always been mutual respect; his interest in my career and writing is genuine, and the first piece of furniture he bought for me was a writing table. Peter's belief in me helped me to have confidence in my own self-expression and goals, and it was very liberating. I discovered people accepted me and felt refreshed by my enthusiasm for life.

By being happy we sow anonymous benefits upon the world.

—*Robert Louis Stevenson*

Of course there were some who rolled their eyes, finding my behavior naive, but there always will be negative people who try to drag us down. Both Peter and I appreciated, from our life experience, how crucial it was for us to be ourselves. I had known since early childhood I was going to live an interesting life, and I was determined never to let being a woman limit me. I felt whole as a human being.

When I worked at Mrs. Brown's decorating firm before starting Alexandra Stoddard Incorporated upon her retirement, we all used our husbands' full names on our calling cards and stationery, with the Mrs. in front. Though this was traditional and socially correct, I felt caged. I couldn't wait to be me, Alexandra Stoddard. But when I ordered more social stationery at Tiffany & Company, I asked for one box to be printed with Mrs. Peter Megargee Brown, with Peter's family crest embossed above the name. When the package arrived, Peter and I sat at the kitchen table and opened the boxes together. When Peter saw the Mrs. Peter Megargee Brown box he froze. "Alexandra, darling, I'm a trial lawyer, you're a designer. It isn't going to do me any good for you to be Mrs. Brown. You are not the first Mrs. Brown, and it means nothing to anyone. You are a designer and a writer and your name is important. Please. When we go to judges' or lawyers' conferences, I will be listed as Peter Megargee Brown and you will be Alexandra Stoddard. When we go to seminars and design symposiums, we will also be listed separately." He meant it and I never once used that box of paper.

You're a happy fellow, for you'll give happiness and joy to many other people. There is nothing better or greater than that.

—*Ludwig van Beethoven*

The will to do, the soul to dare . . .

—*Walter Scott*

Because women in his generation always assumed their husbands' names, Peter's friends still address correspondence to Mr. and Mrs. Peter Megargee Brown, but I realize I can't change them. When they introduce me as Alexandra Brown at parties, I just smile and say, "Hi, I'm Alexandra Stoddard, married to Peter Brown." Peter was wise and firm and I'm appreciative. (Anyway, other than Peter, garden soil, coffee beans, chocolate, and eighteenth-century wood, I loathe brown. My mother's maiden name was Green, and we used to joke, "If you want to change your name be Green, but Brown won't do for a designer and writer." Besides, my mentor was *the* Mrs. Brown, Peter's mother was an angel, and I didn't want to be redundant.)

I love the day.

— *Peter Megargee Brown*

We're all outer directed to a degree, and we're sensitive to what others think of us, but we shouldn't look at life through other people's eyes. Dr. Eric Butterworth believes we must live in the consciousness of inner-centered love, not to be loved, but to be in the process of "dynamic force" so love can freely flow through us. When we live in the spirit of inner-directed love we're less concerned with where we fit in with others and more concerned with how we constructively fulfill ourselves. When we fail to be ourselves we will always feel empty. Then we're at risk of becoming chronically jealous and envious of others, when what we really want is to connect to others with our real selves; that's the only connection that's really meaningful. We know that ultimately we can only live by our own true character and values.

There are some people who have the quality of richness and joy in them and they communicate it to everything they touch. It is first of all a physical quality; then it is a quality of the spirit.

— *Thomas Wolfe*

In her *Advice to a Young Wife from an Old Mistress,* Michael Drury, speaking honestly of marriage, said, "Trust your instincts. One pays a terrible price for a system or rule of authority that will always tell one what to do, and what is worse, what to think. The loss of insight is the blackest of all losses."

I'll never forget my mother whispering some parental advice to me as I left to go on my first honeymoon: "Let him win [at tennis], dear. Don't beat him." That wouldn't have been like me. Instead of losing, I let myself win. We must always let our true selves win.

Romantic Eccentrics

Being myself means being shamelessly in love with life, with every possible experience of beauty, pleasure, and spiritual enlightenment. I am an incorrigible romantic. Some might even say I'm eccentric in the specificity and intensity of my loving ways. We all tend to be eccentric to a degree. Being able to express our exclusive, particular pleasures is an important part of being true to ourselves. Each one of us has our own experience of life's romance.

Some people are so loving they charm birds from the trees.

The remarkable concert cellist, Pablo Casals, at the age of ninety-three, spoke of how he lived his love affair with life. "For the past eighty years I have started each day in the same manner. It is not a mechanical routine, but something essential to my daily life. I go to the piano, and I play two preludes and fugues of Bach. . . . It is a sort of benediction on the house. But that is not its only meaning to me. It is also a rediscovery of the world of which I have the joy of being a part. It fills me with awareness of the wonder of life, with a feeling of the incredible marvel of being a human being. The music is never the same for

Love itself is eternally young and always manifests some of the folly of youth.

— *Thomas Moore*

me, never. Each day it is something new, fantastic and unbe-
lievable."

Can we all experience this great participation in the miracle
of life? Absolutely. Life is miraculous for everyone who is open
to its wonders and genuinely wants to live in the consciousness
of divine love flowing through them. All we have to do is *be*, and
not block this force. Eric Butterworth teaches us, "Don't get in
the way of love." Love is inexhaustible. I believe we have
enough of love's energy to love every
flower, cloud, sunset, song, child, friend,
and person we open up to in a loving, radiant, receptive attitude.

*To be a lover is not to
make love, but to find
a new way to live.*

—*Paul La Cour*

I know many passionate people. My
dear friend and decorating client Kenny
had an unquenchable thirst for life. He
died waiting for a heart transplant at the
age of fifty, living in love until the very end. Kenny was off the
charts with his impractical, gutsy, theatrical, flamboyant, and
juicy attitude toward life. When we were designing colors for
the rafters and beams in the atrium of his office building, we
gave the painter a box of raspberries, and Kenny instructed him
to mash them on a white plate so he could see the exact color
to stain the beams, trusses, and wooden framework; we kept
comparing the stain to this delicious mixture. Cookie, the local
paint doctor, mixed Japanese pigments and concocted this marvelous crushed raspberry color for us. Kenny loved color everywhere, in his garden, in his home, and in his office. He wanted
his world to be cheerful and drenched with light.

One of my other favorite romantic eccentrics is my friend
Ruth. To Ruth all the world is a stage. When she walks into a
room her presence is always felt, filling us all with delight. Ruth

must change her clothes eight times a day because every time you see her she's wearing another, more colorful display. She wears flowing cotton dresses and ties colorful bandannas around her bountiful brown hair. She always polishes off her outfit with a piece of shiny gold, brass, or silver jewelry, perfectly reflecting her inner radiance. Whatever she selects to wear is a direct expression of her mood, her sense of pleasure in the moment, and her appreciation for the day. She's a hopeless romantic.

Make happy those who are near, and those who are far will come.

—*Chinese proverb*

My dear friend June goes "over the top" in seeking pleasure for pleasure's sake. We met in 1963 when I was asked to help her decorate her new apartment in New York, and we've been close friends ever since. June and her husband of fifty years, Randolph, now live in Bermuda when they're not traveling to an exotic, spicy place. Their island home is their paradise, and their gratitude is sublime.

A man doesn't have to be an angel to be a saint.

—*Albert Schweitzer*

June lives inside a colorful cloud, floating in a heavenly blue sky. She greets each new day with joy. Her favorite words are "divine" and "tacky," and she uses them to describe just about everything. She simply wants the whole world to stop acting badly (tacky) and be more loving (divine). Most of us have oscillations, swinging back and forth between our higher and lower self, but June is so radiant with the energy of love, she rarely wavers from her loving path.

Every afternoon between five and six o'clock, June and Randolph leave their beautiful house and drive ten minutes to

Coral Beach, one of the most dazzling, dramatic seascapes in the world. There they sit on a terrace, sip a refreshing cold drink, and privately absorb the majesty. "We can't miss a day, Sandie. It just wouldn't feel right. We come here every afternoon so we can see the sky and water meet, the sun dancing on the waves, and the cotton clouds sketching animals and people against the azure atmosphere. We just feel so appreciative we want to absorb every ounce of this magnificence." And they do.

We can only learn to love by loving.

—Iris Murdoch

June and Randolph never get bored with the view at Coral Beach. "Sandie, we come here as different people each day," June says. "The scene looks new every time we sit and look out. We feel as though we are the luckiest people in the world." Randolph adds with a chuckle, "You better believe it." Just as each morning Mr. Casals gave his benediction at the piano, a mystic begins his day in meditation, and June and Randolph return to the rhythms of the eternal waves crashing to the coral shore, and experience the sun setting on the sea. Whole galaxies are mysteriously revealed when we give in to our romantic spirit, bathing the common in a spiritual glow, pulsing with a transcendent universal energy and divine presence.

Let no one ever come to you without leaving better and happier.

—Mother Teresa

June loves color more than anyone I know, and when we decorated together, everything was always "divine" and never "tacky" because we share the same passion for colors from a seascape, a walk in the woods, a flower garden, and food. June wears paintbox colors. Daffodil-yellow patent leather shoes and wild patterned chromatically intense dresses are staples of her wardrobe. But the most colorful, endearing part of June is her refusal to act her age. She is still daddy's little girl and sees life as a seven-year-old at her birthday party. Her family and friends are her presents. We all know wholeheartedly that June loves us, and because of this we are lifted up to her rainbow cloud where her view of life is awesomely beautiful. For her, living in love is a fact of life.

The words of journalist Ray Sahelian capture the spirit of Casals, Kenny, Ruth, and June and Randolph: *Happiness is the serenity that permeates you when you are profoundly at peace with yourself. It is that overall bubbling feeling that all is well, and that it's great to be alive!*

Perhaps we all cannot live the lives of these people but we can learn from their timeless approach to life. Each one has a unique way of expressing a deep, abiding love of life with wellsprings of satisfactions that are sustaining even when life's climate is stormy.

Whenever there's a choice of suffering because something has gone wrong or turning that suffering into an opportunity to find delight, I go straight for the turnabout, no matter how quirky. Several years ago, after falling off a ladder, I had to have knee surgery. Instead of walking around with exposed ugly ace bandages wrapped around my knee, I began wearing colorful exercise tights to hide them. Our granddaughter Julia, at the age of nine, told me point blank, "Alexandra, I'd worry about you if I ever saw you in boring nude

> *How far you go in life depends on your being tender with the young, compassionate with the aged, sympathetic with the striving and tolerant of the weak and the strong. Because someday in life you will have been all of these.*
>
> *—George Washington Carver*

stockings. When I look in your drawers I'm reminded of a box of crayons. Your wild tights are so you."

Whenever Julia and I are together, she plans what I'm going to wear. She usually begins with the stockings, and then tries to find scarves, blouses, skirts, or slacks to pull it together.

The good life, as I conceive it, is a happy life. I do not mean that if you are good you will be happy—I mean that if you are happy you will be good.

—Bertrand Russell

Several years ago I bought a Day-Glo, acid-green silk suit. I'd had a suit exactly this color with white polka dots that I bought in the early eighties in London. But in one of our closet "de-thuggings," Alexandra put it in the thrift pile. "This color won't do, Mom," she informed me. "The bubble-gum pink one with white polka dots is acceptable, borderline, but this green has had its day." When I found this same color again, among all the dull colors surrounding it on the rack, my heart leaped. *Wait until Alexandra sees this. I'll shock her with another vulgar, raw green suit,* I thought, smiling. Yes, Alexandra will get a kick out of this because she knows her mom loves to be slightly over-the-top. That's who I am.

Love grows out of this pleasure in sensory delight, and it's an expansive energy, helping us grow into openness and readiness for life. Only you can motivate yourself to love by putting loving energy into action. In *Emotional Intelligence,* Daniel Goleman writes, "A related keystone of character is being able to motivate and guide oneself, whether in doing homework, finishing a job, or getting up in the morning." When you put vigor into whatever you do, you experience more delight in life because of your focused enthusiasm.

Soothing Ourselves

Once when I was in a hospital with a loved one who was critically ill, I called a friend for emotional support. John told me, "The patient will be cared for by the best doctors and nurses available. You have to take care of your *self*." Frightened by the thought of death, I cried, "How?" "Read over some of your own books. Listen to the words you give your readers," he answered. Immediately I understood I needed a little isolation from the patient, to be by myself to regain my strength, to become whole again so I could be a resource, a source of positive loving energy. After our conversation, I went to the coffee shop and sat for a while, and then browsed through the gift store where I bought a yellow slicker for $5.99 and a card of a rose trellis in Avignon, France. I wrote a love letter to my ill loved one, and by the time I returned to his room I was practically skipping along the shiny vinyl floor.

The most important decision of our lives is to redirect our energies toward a more positive attitude. This is a life-transforming step.

We learn not to give away more than we have. My spiritual mentor John Coburn believes we need a great deal of time to be alone to think, meditate, read, and write. This is the self-affirming, loving way to balance ourselves so we don't become overwhelmed or discouraged by all the sadness surrounding us. It is not sinful to reinforce a love of life through caring for ourselves. If we don't pay attention to our *self*, we become needy and others have to take care of us because we're incapable of doing so. We lose our freedom as we become increasingly dependent. But when we do whatever is required to feel joy, we don't fall into the trap of feeling sorry for ourselves. We feel the opposite. We feel blessed.

Last year when a friend died in a tragic automobile accident, the first thing I did was buy some flowers and lovingly arrange them. As I licked my salty tears, all the happy memories of Mark Pescatello, a master mason who had become a true friend to Peter and me in Stonington Village, flashed before me. More than six thousand people tried to get into St. Michael's Church in Mystic for his funeral. Our entire village loved Mark, who was also our town treasurer. He loved himself, his Lord, his wife, his three daughters, his community, the football team he coached, his Harley Davidson, and above all, he loved every moment of life. A friend commented, "No one ever saw Mark without a smile on his face. And through his facial energy, his happiness sparkled, his eyes dazzled, and he glowed." Some people seem to have a higher octave of loving energy than others, and Mark's love wavelengths will continue to burn brightly throughout eternity. He was a source of radiant light, and that radiance will never be snuffed out in all of us who love him.

> *To be healthy, be happy. Move toward pleasure as often as you can. Between your periods of work, get relaxation and pleasure. Happiness is not just a luxury, but a necessity.*
>
> —*Martin Rush*

One day Mark noticed Peter on his tiptoes struggling to put a flag in the bronze socket screwed onto the clapboard front of the cottage. (The socket has to be a certain height in order for the flag to fly above the picket fence.) Mark returned two hours later, having dug up some melon-colored granite from a farmer's field, and placed the two giant plinths under the flag flapping in the sea air. Every morning we step up and put the flag in its socket; we feel we're on a throne we affectionately call Mark Rock. He wouldn't consider being paid for his work or the stones. On another occasion he saw my face wrinkled in pain as I held my right elbow with my left hand, dripping ice. Instantly he knew what was wrong. I had tennis elbow and had seen a hand surgeon in New York who suggested I dictate my books because of this pain. I could no more dictate my books than Mark could give up his role as master mason of our village. He returned in his brilliant white truck carrying an elbow strap with a water solution inside that he said would relieve the pain. After he helped me put it on, miraculously my smile returned. Mark felt my pain and wanted to help. That's love.

We attract hearts by the qualities we display; we retain them by the qualities we possess.

—*Jean-Baptiste Antoine Suard*

I framed the snapshot of his wife Jennifer and him sitting on the stone meditation bench he built for me in the garden. Mark's presence is everywhere in our cottage. From the old bluestone on our sidewalk to the Zen garden, the round terrace and our bedroom fireplace, his hand and heart bring us daily joy. I put a huge, over-the-top bouquet of delphiniums in a cobalt blue pitcher on the stone bench and smiled. *Yes, Mark is here; he is everywhere.*

We need a certain kindness and generosity to ourselves before we learn kindness and generosity to others.

—*Lin Yutang*

Daniel Goleman advises that in order to be emotionally intelligent we have to be able to soothe ourselves—to know how to comfort and restore ourselves when we're having a hard time. We can develop our inner resources so that we have a reservoir of strength and loving spirit to draw on when we're having difficulty. Soothing ourselves lets us maneuver through tough times until we reach a better place. When you know how to soothe yourself, you've learned how it feels to be soothed, and you will move toward pleasure instead of penetrating deeper into your pain.

For without the private world of retreat man becomes virtually an unbalanced creature.

—*Eleanor McMillen Brown*

Sometimes just knowing how to please ourselves will change the way we feel, lifting us up from our uneasiness. I love to spend time alone, and if I'm upset for whatever reason, I retreat because I know that I can soothe myself; at least I won't raise my voice. It's a great comfort to know I always have a place where I can go to heal, no matter how grave the situation around me. In this quiet solitude, I can get in touch with my inner strength.

Solitude is how I replenish myself. If I sense anxiety coming on, I stop, clear my head and just *be*. I know how to redirect myself to find comfort and inspiration: to flowers, to natural beauty, sensory delight, the vibrancy of color, the infinity of the heavenly blue sky, and to water. I became enamored with life as a toddler, filled with adoration for the grass beneath my toes, the air, the ancient stone wall, the red barn, and the yellow farmhouse. Smelling the rambling rose bushes, climbing over the picket fence, running naked under the sprinkler, having a watermelon seed fight, shooting waves at the beach, reaching the sky on a swing, blowing bubble gum as big as balloons, picking apples, and making

The happiest person is the person who thinks the most interesting thoughts.

—*William Lyon Phelps*

a pie: These are poignant memories that bolster my spirit to this day. Beauty, color, and light will always be "love expanders" for me. I seek sensual experiences and quiet, so I can hear the wind, the song of birds, and laughing gulls, and children at play.

What we do to love and care for ourselves is different for everyone. Sometimes I need a swim. When my favorite aunt Betty, who took me around the world, died, I swam for several hours. When I'm working through something serious, I love being physical. I'll iron, rinse out my rainbow of colorful stockings, prune the garden, or go for a walk. I usually don't find talking valuable because I know the truth is inside me. Sitting alone, puttering around the house, arranging flowers, gardening, changing the bed sheets, polishing a table surface, orga-

So meditation is not an activity of isolation but is action in everyday life which demands cooperation, sensitivity and intelligence.

—J. Krishnamurti

nizing the desk, taking time to think always clears the cluttered mind, and I emerge refreshed. A hot soak in the tub, a cool swim at the beach, a romantic meal, or reading superb literature usually work their magic; I feel the spirit within confirming, affirming, and blessing the gift of the present, of being alive and mentally, physically, and spiritually whole.

I have learned the art of making time for solitude, when I can temporarily let go of my obligations and be still within myself. I have been a student of Eastern philosophy since I was a teenager, and it has always helped me maintain inner peace. I'm not naturally drawn to nervous, stressed-out, anxious personalities, but I've trained myself to be Zen when I'm in their presence. And I'm always able to walk into an empty room and find space to breathe deeply and return to a calmer, better state.

We all must carve out tranquil time to nurture and love ourselves because we deserve to keep in the dynamic flow of love, in touch with our creative powers. I've never felt guilty about my happiness. We've been given this mysterious gift of life, and each of us has the rich potential to increase our capacity to love and live a richer, fuller life. Anytime we are not ourselves, for whatever reasons, no one can bring us back but ourselves. Wholeness depends entirely on being in a loving consciousness. You are loved because you have divinity inside you as your essential nature. Everything you do to increase your loving self, removing the gridlock of confusion, brings you in closer touch with the vision of pure love.

Meditation simply means thinking, but thinking with a certain spirit.

—*John Bowen Coburn*

You can't try to love someone, but you can practice being in a loving awareness. You can create a loving environment where others will feel loved and accepted. You can see the world through loving eyes and be astonished at the beauty in front of your nose. Not everyone is equal in this respect; some people are more in touch with their higher spirit than others. But all the answers are inside each one of us. We must regularly take time to be alone so we can relate to people on a more loving level. When we refresh ourselves in solitude we absorb a deeper source of divine inspiration, and can become an influence for good in a troubled world.

We are born for love; it is the principle of existence and its only end.

—*Benjamin Disraeli*

Many people get so caught up in the rush and push of life they become exhausted and begin to believe loving oneself or others requires effort. Love should not be exhausting; love is a strengthening force. Blocking it, denying it, making excuses is stressful. No one is ever responsible for someone else's misguided or negative thoughts. We can't control what others do to us, but we can regulate how we react. The more we love, the more love we receive, and by accepting ourselves as we are, we're open to more love. I may not get along with some people, but I still try to send love toward them, rather than anger or dislike. When we love our life and have the courage to live authentically, we will have times when we have to stick up for our rights. Even though most of us don't like to be confrontational, certain behavior in others is unacceptable. However, when we're alone to think things through rationally and reasonably, we know what's important and we stay focused and on our path, because we value love completely, no matter what the exterior circumstances are. Inside us we grow to know how central love is to our well-being.

> *The way one experiences others is not different from the way one experiences oneself.*
>
> —*Erich Fromm*

During an ecumenical service I attended many years ago, as the lights were dimmed, everyone was silent, and for three minutes each person was left to focus inwardly. I was so moved by this powerful experience, I suggested to an Episcopalian minister that he consider instituting the same practice in his urban parish church. My enthusiasm must have been contagious, because he did build three minutes of silent darkness into his sixty-minute Sunday service. The first time, the congregation was taken by surprise and thought there had been a blackout!

> *I make love with my brush.*
>
> —*Auguste Renoir*

Releasing Our Spirits to the Here and Now

The American artist-teacher Robert Henri expressed a universal truth when he concluded, "We will be happy if we can get around to the idea that art is not an outside and extra thing; that it is a natural outcome of a state of being; that the state of being is the important thing."

The practice of meditation reconnects us to our pure state of being. When we meditate, we release ourselves from the persistent pull of external reality—where we are often pulled away from ourselves—and become mindful of our inner state of being. In meditation we learn what it feels like to be alive just in this moment; we learn to love the essence of life that is our very being.

Every moment and every event of every man's life on earth plants something in his soul.

— *Thomas Merton*

Any form of quieting the mind and becoming centered reduces stress. Meditation doesn't necessarily mean sitting lotus style, eyes closed, chanting. There are many ways to reach a meditative state. I meditate whenever I'm alone, quiet, not participating in other people's demands on my time. In these moments of solitude I'm able to muse, think, wait for ideas to surface. The silence allows free association; we unwind, relax, our breathing becomes regular, and a divine peacefulness comes upon us. This loving state of being is available to anyone who takes time to reflect on love and beauty.

Because of my training and experience, I'm now able to get into a flow state whenever I give myself the gift of time.

Whether I'm at the kitchen sink, having a bath, lying in bed before I go to sleep at night, sitting quietly in an antique rocking chair, sitting at my Zen desk, looking at all the meaningful, colorful objects of my affection, I can dwell in this larger space, this higher power lifting me into a place of harmony.

Many people are afraid to be alone, to face the void. But all enlightenment requires this solitude, and if you deprive yourself of it you will not be living as satisfying a life as possible. I would be only half alive if I didn't shut out the rest of the world sometimes, looking at the clouds or painting a box or basket with no interruptions.

Be in reality what we would appear to be. . . . All human virtues increase and strengthen themselves by the practice and experience of them.

—Socrates

Several years ago Peter and I realized that we both wanted to have more time to contemplate, to read and reflect. People's schedules are too crowded. There are too many business demands on top of family responsibilities, as well as social pressures that can eat away at your ability to live in love. Whether I'm wrapping a present, writing a note to a child, or making iced tea for friends, the little rituals I perform are all part of meditation. Ultimately, when we feel we are losing our Zen, we can learn to get into the flow of love, to bring ourselves to a place where we will exude love in all situations. We may not be wealthy or artistic, but we can all learn to be kind and caring, to open our hearts to allow others to enter in.

I was in love with loving.

—Saint Augustine

Paradoxically, I never feel more connected, more in the center of the dynamic force of love than when I give myself these times to be quiet and meditative. Meditation has made me mindful of love as the divine force in my life and my feelings of connectedness to the whole universe.

Be here now.

—*John Lennon*

One evening last year I went to bed after dinner and kept my eyes open, looking up at the moon and stars. I felt cozy, protected, and peaceful, reflecting on the glorious day where I had felt vibrantly alive. I thought about many things, envisioning family and friends, the day's activities. This trance lasted several hours, and when I did finally fall asleep, my dreams seemed supernatural, full of dazzling colors, light, and vitality. Gardens were ablaze with growth and brilliance and I was full of adventure. When I awoke I felt refreshed, as though returning from an exotic vacation without having had the bumps, delays, and expense.

Enthusiasm for Life

Elegance, order, beauty, and joy are available to us every day of our lives. We don't need anything that is not within our reach. It is our spirit that moves us to love what is wonderful in life. In his masterpiece, *A God Within*, Dr. René Dubos speaks insightfully of the durability of a passion for life:

The professional and classical Greeks symbolized the hidden aspects of man's nature, in particular the forces that motivate him to perform memorable deeds, by the word entheos—a god within. From entheos is derived "enthusiasm," one of the most beautiful words in any language. Many people today may no longer believe in the divine origin of inspiration, but there are few who do not retain the ancient and almost mystical faith that enthusiasm is the source of creativity.

Nothing is a burden when you approach life with passionate enthusiasm. When your energy is focused on appreciation, you see with more loving eyes and feel with a more loving heart. The sun on your vase of white tulips is a cause to rejoice. The landscape painting on your bedroom wall delights you. Love's potential is everywhere: in the sweet, heartbreaking music of a Beethoven string quartet, made more poignant by your knowing he was deaf but would lie on the floor to feel the vibrations; when a gentle breeze on a warm summer night caresses your bare shoulders; in acts of generosity; reading in a big cozy chair near a roaring fire; when caring for a child; when you write a letter to someone you miss; when you decorate your home with beauty and meaning; when you look at old photographs; when you have tea with a friend; when you read the wisdom and insights of Emerson, the poetry of Emily Dickinson; and when you sit and meditate, experiencing the breath of life within you.

It is good to love many things, for therein lies true strength; whosoever loves much, performs and can accomplish much, and what is done in love is well done.

—Vincent van Gogh

Dancing and just moving around are guaranteed to boost my loving energy. Sometimes, when I hear a song I love on the radio, one I think of as one of Peter's and my songs, I'll start dancing and feel intense, pure joy. I turn up the music, put on a pair of ballet slippers, and dance around the house. Sometimes while I'm doing housework I'll turn on some sentimental music, even splash on a bit of Peter's cologne and twirl around the house, cleaning.

Reading is central to my life. Literature fills my soul with wonder and enthusiasm. I'll never forget my chance introduction to some of the greatest writers I've ever read. Many years ago, I had packed a poor selection of books for a vacation and couldn't force myself to read them; I ended up reading the girls' summer reading lists, including such luminaries as Jane Austen, Edith Wharton, Madeleine L'Engle, and Louisa May Alcott. You have so much great reading to look forward to if you haven't read works by these writers.

Let those love now, who never loved before; Let those who always loved, now love the more.

— Thomas Parnell

I spend as much time as I possibly can in libraries, reading and writing. Since I never went to college, books have been my teachers, my way of completing a liberal arts education. I continue to be astonished at the fun Peter and I have discussing literature, reading out loud to each other, comparing writing styles and sharing the insights we've accumulated over our collective lifetimes so far. I know we will never bore each other if we continue to keep our minds sharp and alive by sharing our passion for books and ideas.

The supreme happiness of life is the conviction of being loved for yourself.

— Victor Hugo

By expanding your enthusiasm and appreciation for life's riches, you build up your collection of inner resources. Love increases within us when we're alert to life's wonders, when we're excited and stimulated by everything—even the difficult lessons life has to teach us. In books, in dancing, in loving what is possible to love, you'll find more of the positive affirmations you need to nurture yourself when your energy needs uplifting.

Joy, understanding, wisdom, beauty, and grace are realistically rechargeable in our lives if we care enough to try. Discover what pleases you. Beyond the boundaries of your mind, find your passion. Once your spirit soars, your raw vitality accelerates and you exude positive energy from every pore of your being. When you feel this awesome vitality within you, you appreciate even the smallest things. Don't wait for love to come from outside you. There is no way to find love if you are "outer centered." Draw love up from within yourself. Loving energy builds on itself, and in the process of finding wholeness in your self, love lifts you onto a joyful path to connect with others in positive, life-affirming ways.

> *All our reasoning ends in surrender to feeling.*
>
> —*Blaise Pascal*

Healing Your Own Heart

I'm often accused of being a Pollyanna. I am. I look for the good in everything because I know that despite what it takes to overcome pain from the past, renewal is always possible every moment because we can all overcome anything we wish to by changing our attitude and perspective. I have faith in our ability to learn to become more loving because when we alienate ourselves from our true self and detach ourselves from others, we begin to decay inside. Living in love is an intensely exciting adventure. As William Wordsworth said, there will be many moments of "giddy bliss."

We often attribute our hurt feelings to how we were treated in the past. We feel we're limited by the examples, or absence, of loving relationships set for us by our parents. My mother was terribly disappointed in my father, and her four children knew it. He evidently had affairs. Who knows whether or not her behavior drove him into the arms of other women? But their problems never caused me difficulty in loving because I never went to bed at night feeling unloved by my mother or father. I'm not suggesting that we don't all have some pain from the past to overcome. Indeed, we do. But we shouldn't allow the past to dominate our present by using it as an excuse for our inability to feel more loving. Any time we ever pass blame on anyone, we are not assuming responsibility for our self. We must learn from the past or be doomed to repeat it.

The life of man is the true romance when it is valiantly conducted and all stops . . . opened.

—Emerson

During my early childhood, I grew up thinking that I could and should make other people happy by conforming to their ways. I wanted to please everyone, particularly my mother. I was surrounded by people who tried to mold me and shape me up. But what I wanted, what I needed to be, was who I naturally was at that time, a tomboy. I was more often covered in dirt from the rough and tumble of the outdoors, climbing trees and mucking around in the garden, than neatly dressed and pristine.

Because of my strict, almost puritan upbringing, when I was young I always tried to fit in. Being different meant trouble, something I didn't want to get into. I toed the line, abided by my parents' rules, always obeying them because I was in constant fear of criticism and punishment. I feared being grounded. My mother felt it was her duty to correct me all the time, even when I was a grown woman. I never let my past define me, but it wasn't until after my mother died that I felt I could truly stand tall and express myself freely, without fear of criticism.

Is not this the true romantic feeling—not to desire to escape life, but to prevent life from escaping you.

—Thomas Wolfe

While I raised my daughters, I also grew increasingly to understand what I always intuitively knew, that the essence of love must flow as freely as possible through each person. I was always a loving person and I don't think my upbringing inhibited my ability to love. I honored my parents, and in this respect I learned to love myself even while I was conforming to rules, regulations, and restrictions. If our love is stuck somewhere in the past, it won't be available to us today. We offer to share our energy with others by being our authentic, loving selves. It is up to us to accept ourselves as we truly are. Perhaps because I was never allowed to be wild as a child, I'm now having fun loving myself and my quirky, unconventional ways. We're always in the process of becoming, and my dual profession as designer and writer supports this; my career is about creating rather than conforming to convention.

Be really whole, and all things will come to you.

—Lao-tzu

At a certain point in our lives we have to find our own core of self and build a life from that center, no matter what our circumstances, no matter how difficult this seems. Once we see that there is a light from within, no matter what, we can protect it and thrive on it. By triumphing over the obstacles—our past being just one of them—breaking down barriers, and opening up new horizons toward loving, we become a channel for loving energy.

Always know it is not our challenges, but our responses to them that continuously shape our lives. As Dr. Mark Epstein revealed in his book, *Thoughts Without a Thinker,* "It is the perspective of the sufferer that determines whether a given experience perpetuates suffering or is a vehicle for awakening."

Mending the Body

Our body is the temple where inner and outer life are brought into harmony. If something in our life is getting us down, one of the best ways of picking ourselves back up from temporary discouragement or too much pressure is with the pleasures of our bodies. How we experience ourselves as physical beings, how we stay in touch with our five senses, our feeling of strength and physical pleasure, has a life-changing effect on our spirits.

Self-esteem is the ability to be loving, supportive, and respectful toward yourself.

What adds to your energy? What makes you feel strong and radiant? What rituals do you perform to show reverence for your physical body? Do you enjoy the smell and feel of shampoo in your hair? Do aromatic lotions and body oils add to your feelings of sensuality? Can you enjoy the many opportunities you have to enhance your feelings of sensual awareness?

I love to walk because of the physical pleasure of being out in the sun, wind, trees, and birds, leisurely meandering, feeling enormous freedom. As I stretch my legs and swing my arms I'm exercising my mind and body, exploring inner and outer thoughts. Henry David Thoreau wrote *Walking* shortly before his death in 1862, stating, "I have met with but one or two persons in the course of my life who understood the art of Walking, that is, of taking walks,—who had a genius, so to speak, for *sauntering*. . . . For every walk is a sort of crusade. . . ." Walking clears the head, stimulates the flow of blood through the body, is a safe exercise, free, and can fit into any schedule. As you are being good to your body, your soul is awakened to a renewed love of life in your body. I've never known anyone who returned home uptight or confused after musing and moving peacefully out of doors.

> *Just to be is a blessing. Just to live is holy.*
>
> *—Rabbi Abraham Herschel*

Thoreau was right when he admitted how restricting a house becomes if you don't regularly leave it. "How womankind, who are confined to the house still more than men, stand it, I do not know; but I have ground to suspect that most of them do not *stand* it at all." Walking is a sensual delight where we breathe in fresh air and expand our thoughts. My godmother Mitzi Christian told me years ago how intoxicating it was to walk near the water in Duxbury, smelling the sea. "Oh, Sandie, I'd return from a walk feeling I could do anything in the world."

> *A man is happy so long as he chooses to be happy and nothing can stop him.*
>
> *—Alexander Solzhenitsyn*

Many people find pleasure and release working out in the gym, though this never quite worked out for me. I did have a trainer for many years, but because of my competitive nature—

my training in tennis and other sports—I tended to overdo it. I realized that working out was not a way for me to be loving to myself. However, I know many people who take great delight in jogging, lifting weights, and exercising on everything from StairMasters to rowing machines, with a sense of ease. Some friends love their aerobics classes; others swear by stationary bikes. But I find my walks, bike rides, and swimming far more appealing. Whatever the means, the pleasure we feel after exhilarating physical exertion is heavenly, one of life's greatest enjoyments, releasing tension and replacing it with a feeling of lightness and power of being.

Your Inner Nature cannot be fooled. If you do not listen to it, you do not understand yourself very much.

—Benjamin Hoff

The strength and flexibility we gain from exercise expands our experience to a greater dimension. I have friends who so enjoy their bodies in their active state that they extend their exercise into their vacations, sometimes taking hiking trips across mountains or biking down country lanes. These friends return from such trips breathless with joy, describing a remarkable feeling of freedom and delight in their physical selves; a feeling of being one with the wind, the sky, and the sea. Sounds refreshingly delicious to me!

We can take full advantage of our body's potential to bring us more opportunities to love life. Through our body's activity we can overcome a blue mood, restore our spirits, and return ourselves to balance when we're feeling whelmed. But we must, of course, never overdo. Working out till we injure ourselves, or worse, trying to remake ourselves by artificial means, including going on dangerous diets or in many cases giving in to unnecessary cosmetic surgery, may be among the most unloving things we can do to ourselves. They're punishment, not nourishment. When we live in the consciousness of love, we should enjoy the process of being in tune with the sensual pleasures of our bodies and not be goal oriented to the point of losing the spontaneous joy of each moment. Climbing stairs is a thrill to me because I've lived in apartments with elevators for most of my life.

The Nature of This Flower is to bloom.

—Alice Walker

When I'm feeling a bit overworked, here's what I do to treat myself with love: Every once in a while I take a personal day and spend it pampering and nourishing myself. I think of this day as a time of rejuvenation. I have no obligations, freeing up my schedule so I can restore my energy and feel my creative juices. I may begin with a massage, followed by a vigorous swim, then settle in with a good book. I've never experienced burnout because I know when to back off and take a break.

Another way I can bring myself right back up when I'm feeling my energy is low is by looking around to see what's new. I go to one of my favorite stores—sometimes I simply enjoy looking at and touching beautiful things—and might buy a bright pair of lime-green stockings or a gaily-colored floral cotton scarf. My passions are far reaching for colorful, pretty things. I can become wild with joy in a stationery store finding blue note cards with matching envelopes lined with fuchsia tissue paper, hand bordered with the same color. I snoop around house stores, on the lookout for a gift I can give our sweet cottage.

Remember that happiness is a way to travel—not a destination.

—Roy M. Goodman

Whether I indulge in green apple glycerin soap for the kitchen or a new white scrubber to make dish washing more fun, I do whatever the spirit moves me to do because this is *my* time. When you have time where you have no real agenda and aren't rushed in any way, you can enjoy meandering, musing, being absorbed in your own thoughts. I can become completely immersed in the moment as I touch dozens of different hand-blown glass swizzle sticks, made in Murano, Italy, and I might purchase one to add to the collection we keep in a see-through pitcher in the kitchen.

Let my heart be wise.

—Euripides

I hunt around in art stores for colorful file folders, paper, colored pencils and pens. I buy vibrant ink and a few pads of my favorite brilliant white paper. Sometimes I go into a children's store and buy plastic rings in neon Lucite, one for me and one for a grandchild. Treating yourself well when you're not feeling one hundred percent is one of the nicest things you can do, and it's very healing. I'd far prefer going to a coffee shop and hanging out over a cappuccino than staying in the house moping, dragging my body from room to room.

The soul is the mirror of an indestructible universe.

— G. W. Leibniz

We have a wise family doctor who doesn't believe his patients should ever "take to the bed." He thinks the best way to maintain your spirits when you're feeling under the weather is to move around because you weaken yourself when you're immobile, and it dampens your spirits.

One day I wasn't my usual self. I got dressed in a flowered suit and went to the dry cleaners. On my way I smiled at everyone in my path and said good morning. Next to the cleaners I bought a bunch of daffodils and walked around with them as I did rather routine errands. When I went to the hardware store to buy a neon chartreuse laundry hamper liner, I noticed for the first time the teeth of the man who waited on me. When he smiled broadly, I saw mostly gold. "You look mighty sharp today, Mrs. Stoddard." "Thanks. I feel good." And I did.

I decided to call a friend to join me for lunch. When I arrived at the restaurant, the waitress put the daffodils in a water glass, and throughout our meal we felt we were in a garden. We're physical beings and what a joy it is. Certainly, no beautiful scarf or Swedish massage will overcome a sad soul or an unhealthy body, but it is one way of heading in the right direction, toward good feelings and loving energy. Take advantage of the gift of your body and all its myriad ways of bringing you back to your loving self, and see how much love you can generate every day.

The First Gift of Love
Goes to You

Light your own fire! Treat yourself as one engaged in a love affair with life. That is the secret. You have the sky, the earth, the sea. You have your interests and passions. You have talents and the ability to create beauty. Be a romantic for yourself. You're alive. You're at the banquet. Celebrate. Create meaningful rituals so you honor each moment more. Be a living spirit of love. Be open to joy. Love is essentially democratic. Love is available to everyone, at any time, regardless of money, position, age, or outward beauty. We provide the heart and soul for living in love by being open to allow this divine force to flow from within, out. Never take anything or anyone for granted, particularly not yourself. Marvel at the wonder of the beauty of nature and always remember what a miracle it is to be alive with all this love potential inside you. We know today of no other earth.

We release love's power through exultation. Each of us can raise our loving energy, elevating our own life to glorify, praise, and honor what is most exalted inside each of us. Some people inspire our loving energy to reach great heights, but we have inside us all that is life enhancing, beautiful, and good.

We need to look at love as the center of our consciousness, as the core of our being. The total experience of life is an inter-relationship between you and others and matter and spirit. Life is a splendid thing *because* of love. When Peter and I went to see my minister and spiritual mentor John Coburn before we married, John looked across his desk and told us that we will love many people in our life together. There is no way we can reduce our love and respect to just one other person. Life should be a love story.

Living in love is the birth of living joyfully.

If you love flowers, you water them. If you love yourself, you take care of your mind, body, and spirit. Because I love Peter so profoundly, I'm able to increase my love capacity to a higher octave in my love for others. All love begins with you. I can sing along with the Beatles while I wash the kitchen floor or do the laundry, "All you need is love. Love is all you need. . . . Yea, yea, yea." And that's the truth.

How do we grow to become more loving? We begin where we are right now to take full responsibility for our own life. No one can make you love them. You don't need to be in love with one person to feel the divine intoxication of love flowing through you. We have the willpower to redirect our energy and channel it toward the light where love will guide and nourish us. A journalist recently asked me in an interview, "If you could have one message, Alexandra, what would it be?" "Love," I answered. Love is our path. Love is our way. We love life on earth through our physical bodies and minds, and by loving our-selves, we are showing appreciation for the gift of life. At birth, each of us is given this divinity to be released from within. Happiness and joy are a result of loving energy. Write a love letter to yourself and you'll see with clearer vision how much you love life.

And love, that grows from one to all.

—Charles Williams

If there is one thing I'm sure about, it is love. Because I have been fortunate in my life so far to be able to love and find meaning, satisfaction, and pleasure in the mere fact that I'm alive, I know with my body, heart, and spirit that when my ener-gies are channeled in love, I am refreshed, filled with grace, and have an abundant feeling of goodness. And in this conscious-ness I connect with Peter, my family, my friends, and you.

If you love others, you treat them with kindness and honor their dignity. When you love anything—a place, an experience, music, art, food—all this love accumulates and becomes absorbed in your consciousness and lifts you up into a higher, more divine place. When you are in this awareness, you no longer have to question what is the meaning of life because the answer is inside each of us, and it is love. The potential to live in love is an art where we all can be the artists. This is the good news.

3.

"Are You Getting What You Wanted?"

. . . if they succeed in loving the distance between them which makes it possible for each to see the other whole against the sky.

— RAINER MARIA RILKE

What Are We Looking For?

The week after returning home from Peter's and my honeymoon I went back to work. I'd taken a few days to organize the movers, and managed to unpack eight or ten boxes. I had color coded the things I wanted to unpack immediately—favorite treasured, sentimental objects, desk accessories, and books that would make Peter's apartment seem more like home right away.

The office was quite busy, so I was back in the thick of work as soon as I stepped through its doors. Returning from a client's Beekman Place apartment, Mrs. Brown and I walked through the shipping room, checking my fabric bin for deliveries, and, without admitting even a hint of fatigue, this eighty-four-year-old grande dame marched up the narrow steps of the townhouse to the showroom. Mrs. Brown often told her assistants, "You have to be in training for life." Resisting the temptation to rest on the oriental mahogany hall bench and put down four canvas tote bags to regain flexibility in my hands, I followed her assured lead up four more steep flights. How could she glide up this staircase, unfazed?

There is comfort in the strength of love.

— *William Wordsworth*

When we reached the fifth floor, she stood on the hall carpet runner, not even holding the iron banister with the brass railing for support, and turned to me. Before anyone could overhear her, she inquired, "Well, Sandie, are you getting what you wanted?"

Laughing, I responded, "*I* am, Mrs. Brown; you'll have to ask Peter that question." Her frankness bewildered me. I walked to my office and over to my desk where I bent down, shedding the tote bags at last. My neck felt tense. As I checked my telephone messages, I noticed my hands were ripples of hot pink and white ridges from lugging marble and tile samples around town. After washing up, I served myself some chamomile tea with lemon, selected a Lorna Doone vanilla cookie, and, upon returning to my desk I muttered to myself, *Hmmm, am I getting what I wanted?* (At that precise moment I wanted a porter to carry my bags. Ah, herbal tea and a nibble on a cookie hits the spot. I felt glad to be back at work. Our client loved all our schemes. In less than a year the job would be completed, and I'd no longer be needed.) As I sank into the seat of my secretarial swivel side chair, hardly a glamorous piece of furniture but efficiently useful, I turned toward the window, gazing out onto the city.

Love is patient and kind; love is not jealous or boastful; it is not arrogant or rude. Love does not insist on its own way; it is not irritable or resentful; it does not rejoice at wrong, but rejoices in the right. Love bears all things, believes all things, hopes all things, endures all things. Love never ends.

—I Corinthians 13:4–8

Next to Brooke, Mrs. Brown was the most supportive of Peter's and my decision to marry. How well I remember her proudly announcing our engagement at a monthly firm meeting. When she asked, "Are you getting what you wanted?" I intuitively sensed she was inquiring, "Are you divinely happy now that you and Peter are one?"

We are all unique, complex beings with secret dreams, fantasies, mysteries, and longings we want to act out in our lives. I believe we are who we are, and, when we are allowed to be our most authentic, vulnerable, real selves, "We've only just begun," as the Carpenters' song goes, to set free the potential electricity buried deep within us, waiting to be released. If we understand the importance of this expansion not only for ourselves, but for our partner, then we have begun to grasp the energy of a lifelong commitment.

Faithfulness is one of the marks of genius.

—*Charles Baudelaire*

So many people tell me frankly they wish they had "caught on" earlier in life, because once you "get it," life becomes a thrilling adventure. After I gave a talk one day entitled "Bringing Nature's Colors Inside Your Home," the chairperson for the lecture luncheon commented how she enjoyed my presentation. "I love flowers the way you do, Alexandra," she told me. "That's why I take so many walks so I can peek into gardens and become lost in the wonder." I'd mentioned in my talk how we can have a garden in full bloom become a personal metaphor for our lives. Accumulatively everything I've ever seen in bloom increases my happiness. I carry these images around with me, visualizing the gardens of my friends who let me take pictures I can use in my talks. Seeing the vibrancy of lush gardens, flower beds in brilliant colors against blankets of grass, trees, and blue sky always reinforces my passion for flowers. One woman asked me how old I was when I developed my positive outlook. I was flattered. I paused and answered, "Three."

While I wasn't specific in knowing what I wanted, I sensed Peter loved me the way I was, that he wasn't here to make me over to fit the image of a woman he may have had in mind. He wanted me to be completely myself. There are many traps women can fall into if their spouse insists on clearly defined, traditional gender roles.

Both of us knew from experience how crucial it is for each person to be allowed the freedom to be who they are, not falling into routines or safe places to ease the challenges of a full life.

Nothing is generous if it is not at the same time just.

— Cicero

Peter loves variety, loathing banal routines and labels as much as I do. We discovered we each enjoy experiencing as much spice in life as possible. We had the relative freedom to choose what we wanted to do together, finding our preferences simpatico, and our personalities and temperaments amazingly similar. I knew I would like to continue to define my life in a variety of different ways, not only in my relationship to Peter, my children or our home, but in my work, always in the process of evolving.

Peter grew up with his father as the patriarch of the family, the bread winner, and his mother a full-time mother, wife, and housekeeper. Peter recognized and honored me for my differences from any woman in his past, allowing me autonomy to express myself in whatever ways I wanted to, bringing me personal fulfillment. He didn't let his own traditional upbringing interfere with what we knew was right for our love to continue to grow. Peter never holds me back. With double thumbs-up, Peter smiles and says, "Go for it. Life is short."

Too often the legal certificate of marriage ends up turning love into a contract where inflexible roles are established by one or both spouses. The couple begins to act in much the same way as people in a workplace do when they perform only in the narrow avenues of their exact job description because their egos or the boss won't allow for any variety of experience and action.

In love the paradox occurs that two beings become one yet remain two.

—Erich Fromm

Is it easier to be yourself outside a marriage? No. In a lifelong commitment you can open up to far greater depths of freedom. Far too many women, unhappily, turn immediately into a housewife rather than a loving companion. In marriage you never know. Habits form, chores need to be done, and so many otherwise intelligent women soon become *house keepers* rather than lovers. As our friendship grew deeper into a commitment, Peter and I were increasingly confident we were capable of a successful marriage. Peter and I view marriage and each other as a union. Union derives from the Latin word *unus*, one. We're in the same situation, we both want to live together in love. Fundamentally we both want the same from life. Whenever a man pressures a woman or a woman asks too much of a man, mutual resistance arises and the two can't truly unite. Peter and I have achieved the qual-

Both of you want to receive and be received.

—Thomas Moore

ity of being one, where we both serve each other, together tending to the matters at hand so each individual's burdens are reduced and a spirit of mutuality binds us closer.

We both acknowledged our pasts, including our mistakes, poor judgments, our prejudices, but tried not to carry emotional baggage into our relationship. Looking back, I realize Peter is the first man I ever trusted completely to know how fiercely independent I am. Most men are threatened by a gutsy, strong woman; but because he wasn't, my independence bloomed after we were married. I really started to mature, adding extra dimensions to our bond. We found more and more how similar our passions were to be free to live complete, exciting lives. (Both of us care more about the books we pack for a vacation, for example, than what clothes we bring.) But, most importantly and paradoxically, by each of us honoring and respecting each *other*, as individual beings, we grew as one.

Fulfilling Mutual Goals

What do we value in an intimate love relationship? Are we doing all we can to encourage our exchange of love?

In *Advice to a Young Wife from an Old Mistress*, Michael Drury goes to the heart of the issue of how to grow in love: "... the principal question is what you want. All other questions—of children, money, home, position, family, work, friends, survival—while legitimate, are derivative; that is to say, without the marriage these questions would never exist, or they would take a very different form. The answers to them will be satisfactory and lasting only after the basic matter of personal wants is faced. If you cannot discern what it is you desire, you grope in a fog of dissatisfactions without really knowing why, and hit out in all the wrong directions."

> *Love is an activity, a power of the soul.*
>
> —*Erich Fromm*

Before training our loving energy to grow and flourish in an intimate, committed relationship, first we must face the truth about our self. No other person is ever responsible for our unhappiness, or our happiness. True love may conquer all, but only when based in real life, and while you acknowledge love's value to you as a unique, individual, evolving being, seeking enlightenment.

Some people are better alone because they're unable to escape the prison of narcissism and selfishness. I know an immature woman who suffers terrible feelings of deprivation in her relationship because she demands so much of her husband, unwittingly leaving him no alternative but to fail her. Brenda expects Tom to read her mind. She assumes he's telepathic, able to detect when she's had a bad conversation with her boss or to sense when she wants time alone with him. On a recent birthday, Tom gave her an expensive bracelet from Tiffany. She was horrified by the gift. She found it gaudy and a gross misreading by Tom of who she was. "I opened the lid of the black case and I burst into tears," Brenda exclaimed. "This was the last straw—everything Tom does is wrong. He doesn't have a clue who I am. He continuously lets me down."

Brenda is lost on love's path because she is not acting in a loving manner. Her rejection of this gift of love is abusive. Tom is a thoughtful, loving soul, not the inept misfit she paints him as being. One might conclude: Not only does she not want to live in love, she rejects being loved.

> *We know of the seven deadly sins. But how many are familiar in this age with the Seven Virtues? Faith, Hope, Charity, Prudence, Justice, Fortitude, and Temperance. Think of all these positives as well.*
>
> —*Peter Megargee Brown*

> *There is no fear in love.*
>
> —*I John 4:18*

This may be an extreme example, but when you think about it you can see how it illustrates a not uncommon reason why some people feel they're not getting the love they want: Unhappiness in love can arise when someone has closed the door to their heart. As the Buddha teaches, "Joy and openness come from our own contented heart." We raise our love to a higher level by seeking what mature love is. This is not a selfish quest, but is based on preservation of integrity and individuality.

Time and time again, those who examine the intricacies of happiness have found the same thing—realistic expectations are among the prime contributors of happiness.

—Geraldine K. Piorkonski

We automatically set ourselves up to be let down when we unfairly place unrealistic expectations on others. When we do this, we're asking others to fulfill some need we ourselves cannot define, making us impossible to please. Sweet Tom is set up from the start as an innocent victim because Brenda is motivated by material needs, treating Tom as an object, not a vulnerable, sensitive soul. Rather than looking at the whole perspective, seeking a higher purpose, understanding Tom as a human being, with divinity, Brenda's empty center casts stones. Who does she think she is to set these artificial standards *for somebody else*? Why does anyone feel justified having expectations about how another human being will satisfy their needs? Anyone who ever feels they can control another person will eventually feel let down, and rightly so. We cannot expect people, even those who love us the most, to bend over backward trying to please us and make us happy.

Being kind is the first order of loving.

—C. Rickert Lewis

Such behavior and placement of blame reflect poorly on us. We need to stop in our tracks, step outside ourselves, and ask, "Do I want to be this person, making others feel uncomfortable, *obliged* to pay attention to me, against their wishes? Do I want others to walk on eggshells around me, out of guilt and fear? Do I want to be virtually impossible to please?"

Love is a little blind; when we love someone dearly we unconsciously overlook many faults.

—Beatrice Saunders

Eastern philosophy invariably brings more light to my center, teaching me that any kinds of cravings or strong desires, if we cannot fulfill them, will cause us heartache, and we ourselves are often the root of our suffering. If we set ourselves up for disappointment by unrealistic expectations that are impossible to fulfill because they involve resources other than our own, surely we'll fall into this trap of failure. When we exercise common sense and understanding, when we have a mutual cause, we'll want to be fair and reasonable, and chances are we'll be able to broaden our perspective and become more realistic. We then add strength for new encounters with others.

A Key Challenge of Love

The truth about love has been with us since the beginning, though it still takes each of us our own time to understand, to believe in and rely on love as the greatest, most powerful force for good available to us as human beings. In the *Nicomachean Ethics*, Aristotle brilliantly summarized a key challenge of love—also identifying the secret to its solution: "Anyone can become angry—that is easy," he said. "But to be angry with the right person, to the right degree, at the right time, for the right purpose, and in the right way—this is not easy."

Indeed, it is hard to use our anger constructively in the interests of supporting our love. An intimate love should not be abused by any strong feelings of displeasure, resentment, or hostility. Do you want your loved ones to bear the brunt of confused, conflicted, and harsh emotions?

Set a high value on spontaneous kindness.

—*Samuel Johnson*

Erich Fromm advises, "Most people see the problem of love primarily as that of *being loved,* rather than that of *loving,* of one's capacity to love." The only time your anger may be justified is where someone actually abuses you. Whenever someone insults you, uses coarse language, or maltreats you physically, you have to be tough minded. Remember the key word: unacceptable. I will not be around anybody for long who is mean spirited, trying to tear me and others down. Life is far too precious; we must always remain courageous in order to protect our integrity.

In *Emotional Intelligence,* Daniel Goleman writes about the situations where couples, feeling their tender emotional buttons aggressively pushed, are propelled into anger that far outstrips the provocation. Goleman aptly calls these incidences "neural highjackings." It's as though an alien has a hold over the nervous system.

These neural highjackings are one of the trouble spots in all intimate relationships. None of us can be 100% loving all of the time. Even the most balanced of us lose it sometimes. I'll never forget the scene I once witnessed at an airport while I was waiting for my flight. A man began screaming at his wife, who had apparently gone for a walk with their daughter and had lost track of time. Mother and daughter were having fun browsing in a gift store and forgot to check their watches. The plane began boarding and the husband went ballistic, fearing they'd miss their flight. He became totally unhinged. His face turned beet red with rage. He was caught up in what Daniel Goleman would call "an escalating scale of misery."

I became tense just witnessing this disturbing scene. The poor woman had made the mistake of enjoying herself with her daughter. If this event at the airport was a true indication of his behavior, the continued journey must have been equally unpleasant. Yes, she had been careless, but certainly she didn't deserve such criticism. As they boarded the aircraft I couldn't help but notice the irony of a banner on the wall above their heads: *Delta Spirit: Commitment, Teamwork and Dedication.* Just what was obviously missing in this relationship.

> *Don't flatter yourself that friendship authorizes you to say disagreeable things to your intimates. The nearer you come into relation with a person the more necessary do tact and courtesy become.*
>
> *— Oliver Wendell Holmes*

I believe this anger is a form of temporary insanity, something we all experience but should never let become a chronic condition. In all our relationships, with ourselves and any other human being, we have a choice about how we direct our energies. A woman Peter and I met in Boston at a seminar told us her father always played cheerful, peppy music whenever one or more of the children was in a bad mood. "Before we knew what was happening to us, we were clicking our fingers and thumping our feet to the beat, clapping our hands, and our frowns curled up into smiles."

Redirecting Energy Toward Love

If love is a positive energy, a tonic in an often toxic, negative world, why aren't more people enjoying a greater amount of harmony and tenderness than they are? Even if a couple feels they're both better off leading separate lives, they can still be friends and love each other. I'm baffled why two people would live with chronic strain and insidious, distressing aggravation. If you're lovable, most people feel your sincerity and respond by giving love back to you. Loving people bring out love in others.

We should look long and carefully at ourselves
Before we pass judgment on our fellows.

—Molière

The disposition of those around us has a profound effect on our mood. I was being interviewed on a radio show in Colorado when a listener called in and said everyone in her family and all her friends are negative. They always point out what's wrong. "What should I do?" The host of the show, a psychologist, shouted into the microphone, "Tell them to drop dead." I suggested, "Give them a wide berth."

Growing up, I was trained to adhere to the belief "If you can't say something nice, don't say anything at all." The loving people who set high standards for me approach life positively, finding appropriate resolutions to situations, and they always try to be fair, caring, and nurturing, no matter how aggravating the situation.

After I turned fifty, I wrote *Making Choices: The Joy of a Courageous Life,* revealing tough choices I've made in my life. I realize I'll continue to make equally difficult ones in the years to come. One decision I have chosen to live by is to set my own boundaries for unloving people, whether they are family members or related in some other way. Tearing down others is a clear signal of mental and emotional ineptness. The power to weaken the emotional stability of another person is strong; just as strong as the opposite, positive effect love and caring can have on another soul.

A sense of duty is useful in work, but offensive in personal relations. People wish to be liked, not be endured with patient resignation.

— Bertrand Russell

I'm no longer a young woman. I've experienced many pains and disappointments along with all the awesome joys and mysteries of fulfilling, loving relationships. I want to try to continue to be a loving person, while never losing sight of reality. There are people who not only don't love me, they wish I would disappear. There is one woman who, every time she sees me, begins her greeting with a derogatory remark: "Oh, you're wearing your pajamas" when I have stretch pants on, or "Are you off on a sail?" when I am wearing a fuchsia windbreaker in a local diner. Once, when we ran into each other in a hotel lobby in Boston, she immediately asked sarcastically, "Are your stockings bright enough?" On another occasion, Peter and I ran into this person, face-to-face, at a reception and she never acknowledged me, talking solely to Peter as though I were invisible.

I've always felt that even if you don't adore someone, you can at least be polite. Manners provide a civil sense of harmony between human beings who otherwise feel awkward with each other. Is it possible to irritate another human being to irrational degrees, so that decency, honor, and civility is not possible? Could it be this woman not only can't stand to see me, but really hates me? But if she doesn't care for me, why does she waste her energy being overtly hostile? What does she have to gain? Perhaps I'll never understand. But what lessons can we learn from her example? What is the reality of her behavior?

Everybody needs more love.

—Daphne Rose Kingma

George Williams, one of the pioneers of the new science of evolutionary psychology, believes "an individual who maximizes his friendship and minimizes his antagonisms will have an evolutionary advantage, and selection should favor those characters that promote the optimization of personal relationships."

If we're with someone whose nature is calculating, and manipulative, and who ultimately tries to pick us apart, innuendo by innuendo, what choice do we have but to retreat? If someone acts viciously to acquaintances, this behavior probably has ingrained patterns that seep into their other relationships, perhaps with children and even in their intimate dealings with a spouse. Each of us knows in our heart when we're hurting someone's feelings because we share a mutual vulnerability and volatility; the behavior is reciprocal, curiously felt by both sides.

Peter and I try to work in tandem toward shared dreams, goals and hopes, filling the moment with love, generally building each other up, minimizing antagonisms. One person's ability to relate to another is the mirror reflection you have inside your own heart and soul. No one tears someone else down without being miserable themselves. I'm so grateful to be able to spend my life with Peter, stimulated by his sunny disposition and his energy, and attracted to his graceful manner. Our relationship compels me to want to be more patient, more just, more tolerant, more loving.

In the years when I raised small children and was going through a divorce I wasn't always Zen-calm. I worried about my children, about money, and about our future. Yet I never lost hope or faith. I said to a nervous friend a few years ago, "Mary, worry is a basic lack of faith." She couldn't believe me, because she felt she had to worry if she truly loved her husband and children. There's no question, we are all concerned. It comes with the territory when we love. But to worry incessantly, to feel uneasy or deeply troubled, to brood, causes one inevitably to feel anxious and distressed, translating quickly into negative energy that could be used in positive ways.

> *If things are ever to move upward, someone must be ready to take the first step, and assume the risk of it.*
>
> — *William James*

Our daughter Alexandra woke up from a bad dream in a blind panic one night because she hadn't heard from her cat sitter. Because she was going to be away for four days, she feared Clayborn and Lesieur would run out of water and food. She called, reached Christina, and all was well. Her anxiety over the situation proved to be unnecessary, but whenever we feel something is wrong, when we're loving, we act. Love is an irresistible force.

> *The greatest part of our happiness or misery depends on our dispositions and not on our circumstances.*
>
> —*Martha Washington*

Peter and I love working out all the dimensions of our union together, maintaining a rapport, being kind, affectionate and appreciative toward each other. Our love is reciprocal, but not with the expectation that we're going to get something in return. We already have the essence of all we could ever hope for or ever have. Together we feel whole, complete.

Some people find this state not in one other person, but through their friends and even through their love of work. When someone is genuinely loving, whether they're interacting with others or alone in solitude, the intangible energy flows in more graceful, sweeter ways in all directions. By stepping back, you can see the nonsense of putting effort into negative states of mind and know that only by *feeling* loving will you discharge and receive loving energy. How can we all move in a more loving direction so our energy is redirected in more positive ways? We can never fairly rationalize reacting to certain situations by insulting and demoralizing another soul.

Life is as fleeting as a rainbow, a flash of lightning, a star at dawn. Knowing this, how can you quarrel?

—Buddha

There are always emotional forces at play, but when our conversations are laden with ire, when we have an annoyed tone of voice and an angry expression, when our whole sense of disgust is displayed on our face, eyes rolling and teeth gritting, we get nowhere except more anxious and tense. Lack of love has permutations and combinations that can be deadly. Some people rush to the grave with clenched fists, livid to the end, rather than maintaining a hand open to the possibilities of love.

No matter what happens, you can always stay in a loving place. Concentrate on how you react to negative situations, knowing love is a divine force for good and any break from this loving energy is self-destructive. When someone really hurts me, I may feel pain and betrayal, but my love does not go away. Love requires us to pay attention to our voice from within. Your inner voice never lies.

Once you're able to feel love in solitude, you can go for a walk or be still in a room or on a park bench until you're Zen again. Don't allow being upset with someone who is unloving reduce your power to remain loving. *Being* yourself by definition means being *loving*. If ever you are in a situation where someone acts badly, don't enter into anything that will misdirect your loving, positive energy into a hissy fit. Pretend you're being taped and that you'll watch the film at a later, calmer time. Being yourself means being awake to your higher self, your spiritual nature, not giving into a lower, dark side.

A friend once said something I'll never forget: "Alexandra, once I looked at another soul and was determined to feel something good toward that person, and my life turned around." That sudden insight comes back to me often as the days pass. Another friend told me about a healer whose gift was the ability to open up his heart and become one with another person and feel where they needed to be healed. Peter's compassion for me and mine for him, reassure each of us we'll always face life's challenges while feeling the joy of living in love together.

Love comforteth like sunshine after rain.

— William Shakespeare

In today's world I sense a frequent tendency for depressed and inert souls to say they cannot bring themselves to emerge from a fur-lined rut. They've grown content in a self-pitying mold. Several years ago Peter and I overheard a man telling his friends about a time in his life when he was miserable. "I'd go to my room, close the curtains, lie in bed, and think awful thoughts. I had everything—a big house, a wife, children, and money and I still felt depressed. I pondered my misery in despair. It got so bad I decided I was going to have to do something. Could I find a way to be happy being sad? I decided I was going to enjoy my misery. I jumped out of bed, ran to the bay window, threw open the curtains, opened the French doors, looked out at my wife and daughter sitting by the pool, walked toward them with a smile and outstretched arms, and hugged them both. The decision to be happy being sad lifted the depression into feeling glad to be alive. Everything is fine now. I've decided to be happy and I am."

A Hand to Hold

As a trial lawyer, Peter's word skills are overdeveloped for domesticity. He's been trained to win all arguments in court and he sometimes participates in our discussions as a litigator rather than a caring companion. Peter has at times tried to defeat me instead of trying to understand my point of view. He knows how to make compelling arguments that can be difficult to dispute; words are so readily available to him that sometimes talking prevents him from listening. During these episodes, I've had to remind Peter that the purpose of our discussions is to deepen our communication and understanding, not to defeat one another. We are not on opposite sides, but love each other and have shared goals.

We all get into this bind of competition with our loved ones. We have to defend ourselves so much in the world that sometimes it's hard to take our gloves off when we come home. Many times when we quarrel we're trying to get the upper hand, when what we really want is a hand to hold.

Can people learn the human emotional skills needed to maintain a healthy, loving relationship? Once two people tear each other apart, is it possible to repair all the damage? Once a couple is capable of collectively letting go of the past, and collaboratively begins to move forward in forgiveness, can there be *true* union between them? Can the trust be restored, or will there be fear of betrayal? When people "make up," do they revert to their natural behavioral patterns whenever things don't seem to be resolved?

I had dinner with a friend after giving a talk at our local Stonington library. Frank was bothered because he felt I had declared divorce justified under certain circumstances in my talk that evening. "Divorce shouldn't be an option," he told me, "you should be able to work things out." In theory, I agreed with him. And I believe that many failed marriages could

The basic ways we feel about each other, the basic kinds of things we think about each other and say to each other, are with us today by virtue of their past contribution to genetic fitness.

—Robert Wright

have been saved if more effort and attention were given to the couple's problems. But I also believe it is a far greater sin to stay legally married when you are destroying each other's dignity, self-esteem, and confidence and ultimately depressing each other's spirit because, after many trials, you are irrevocably incompatible.

We do have the remarkable ability to change, to live in a more loving consciousness, but we must want to. When we learn how to become more loving, we respond to what life deals us, including the darkest storms, more effectively and rationally. The first step is to become mindful of how we react to difficult situations. When someone upsets us, do we attempt to hurt them back? Do we want them to suffer more? When people, including children, don't feel loved enough, they sometimes act in unloving, needy ways to try to get our attention. But mature love doesn't naturally work that way. Love is essentially our true nature emanating from our heart, soul, and spirit, boundless, sundrenched, luminous, and vibrant. This energy is self-sustaining, multiplying infinitely each second we are in a loving state.

> *Love is all we have,*
> *the only way that*
> *each of us can help*
> *the other.*
>
> —*Euripides*

We must figure out ways to get in touch with our higher power, and work on directing our energies in positive, life-sustaining ways. Because each of us may be born with a genetic predisposition toward personality extremes, it is wise to accept who we are and work to improve our perspective and attitude. This way we are as emotionally and spiritually healthy as we can be, based on the reality of nature as opposed to nurture. If mental well-ness and ill-ness are the outcome of a combination of nature and nurture, it is logical to want to work on the areas we can control. Every experience, each person in our life, will accumulatively have an effect on our spirit.

By deliberately making a commitment to be around good people, caring, nurturing souls who build us up, who are empathetic, who accept us as we are, chances are we will elevate our thoughts to a loftier place.

I'm grateful I've had some loving role models, beginning with Grandfather Johns, a minister, Aunt Betty Johns, an international social worker, John Coburn, a minister, Mitzi Christian, an artist, Phyl Gardner, an artist and teacher, and Mrs. Brown, an interior designer. These people taught me by example how to increase my passion for life. When there are older people whom you admire in your life, you literally look up to them and try to emulate them all through life. You're on tiptoes, stretching yourself to greater heights. You stand on the shoulders of giants.

While John Coburn is now the only living person among the giants who helped shape my life, the others are present in my soul, continuing to inform my thinking and actions. I love these heroes, and they obviously love me because we connect in profound ways. Aunt Betty not only took me around the world when I was an impressionable teenager, she also invited me to live with her the first semester I was at the New York School of Interior Design in New York in 1959. During this time I observed her earnest correspondence with more than five hundred people from around the globe. She embraced the world with love.

It is love, not reason, that is stronger than death.

— Thomas Mann

Think about the power a single smile can have on a complete stranger. A smiling face spreads joy to others. I believe you can think a loving thought about someone and mysteriously this love, as a prayer, is transmitted and felt by the person at whom the love is directed. When you love me, even though I don't hear you say "I love you" with my ears, I feel it intuitively.

Fighting over "Little Things"

We all have our little situations with toothpaste blobs around the sink, rings around the bathtub, spots on the tablecloth, and idiosyncrasies about what we want for supper. We have personal habits that could be irritating to the other, however strong our love for each other. Peter and I have a little difference about the bathtub in the cottage. Peter cannot resist the temptation to fill our deep bathroom tub all the way to the top and empty at least half a bottle of rare bubble bath into it. As a result he often floods the bathroom floor. I once told him in a moment of exasperation that either we needed a new tub or I needed a new husband. Peter has lots of areas where his passionate nature sends him overboard. He loves to build bonfires in the fireplace. He wouldn't call them that, but they are, and they usually set off the smoke alarm.

> *When you differ with a man, show him, by your looks, by your bearing, and by everything that you do or say, that you love him.*
>
> —*Senator Paul Douglas*

As lovers, we should try to avoid the pitfalls of trivial irritations and disruptions. It's never worth fighting because your spouse forgot to bring home the garlic. How many discussions about chores deteriorate into "laundry lists" about who did what for whom?

But these arguments about "little things" may not be about little things at all. Sometimes, petty squabbles can be about a more serious frustration. Tears about bathtubs and groceries may occur when loving communication is blocked. Instead of telling one another what you feel, you may spin your wheels saying provocative, defensive things, getting you deeper into the black hole of miscommunication and alienation. Whenever two people are very close, it can be difficult at times to talk openly to each other because so much is at stake. It can be frightening to say what you really feel at times for fear of deeper hurt or rejection. Whenever you lash out offensively or puff up indignantly at each other you can sever your connection, like a telephone gone dead.

Everyone knows the feeling of running into a wall when you're trying to convey how you feel to your lover. Regardless of what you say, your real meaning often will not be heard. But something you're doing or saying may be exacerbating the problem. Listen to your tone of voice and choice of words. One of the most destructive ways of miscommunication is to accuse each other of failing *entirely* rather than simply mishandling a specific situation. At these times, the person you love may air his grievances in a litany of complaints.

Faith has need of the whole truth.

—Pierre Teilhard de Chardin

Because your lives are so entwined, you both become dispirited, stymied, and defeated.

Peter often hears his divorce clients complain, "He always . . ." or, "She never . . ." How can just a few little words make such a big difference between two grown people? They can. Speaking in such fatal terms, as "always" and "never" expresses a hopelessness about the other person, splintering the relationship, perhaps permanently. Rather than accusing our spouse of not listening to us, we can suggest how we would like to be treated in the situation at hand. Often, the source of our problems is that we really don't ask for what we need.

Love is a great teacher.

—Saint Augustine

The Greek philosopher Socrates practiced the method of trying to arrive at truth by asking incisive questions. We need to ask ourselves a series of questions before placing any blame. By identifying exactly what we feel hurt about and what we need, we often find that our lover actually wants to be there for us. Many times they'll admit they didn't really have a clear idea why we were so anguished in the first place or what they had done to provoke us. Once they know, they no longer feel globally accused, and can then be free to generously give us tenderness and love. When we listen to our love as they try to tell us about their feelings, we discover something new about them and we feel less personally attacked. Use softer, more loving words so others can listen more tenderly; you will usually find a more sympathetic ear.

Staying Connected

During a discussion about relationships our daughter Brooke recently said, "Marriage should not be a correctional institution." That's true. Peter and I have found ways of talking about our concerns as well as problems without belaboring them, a powerful means for us to keep our loving energy flowing.

A heart and spirit centered in love shine brilliantly even in darkness.

Whenever crises do arise, and they will, more love, empathy, and compassion is needed than when things are going well. Peter and I try to stick together, no matter what tragedies or situations we have to face.

When Powell had to have open heart surgery, Peter and I went to Chicago on a Monday to be with him during the operation on Tuesday. Our return tickets to New York were for Thursday afternoon, but Wednesday night I looked at Peter, burst into tears, and begged him to stand by Powell and me "to see this through." I was firm in telling Peter I couldn't leave my brother, but he was torn because he had so many legal obligations. I had to plead with him. In a transitional moment his eyes softened, he held both my hands, and asked, "Do you really want me to stay, darling?" "Angel, I need you. Please." "All right. I'll stay with you. I love you." Not knowing what this commitment meant, his love grew exponentially. That Friday, the day after we were scheduled to return to New York, my brother died with us at his bedside along with his wife and children.

When you live in the midst of loving energy, you stay supportive of each other in times of sadness and grieving, situations outside our sphere of influence. Love is always available, no matter what inconveniences you may encounter. Love draws you in so you are in the right place at the right time for the right reason. Being able to grow more loving and kind when your spouse is suffering is the best way to live life without regrets. Be determined to stick together through thick and thin because this is love in action. When you mutually work through a situation so you both feel more united in the end, the force of love cannot be blocked.

We must strengthen, defend, preserve and comfort each other.

—John Winthrop

On one soulful weekend, Peter and I decided to take a delicious nap in front of our large living room fireplace. We were at home on a sensual, intimate date, both on the same wavelength. All that kept us from starting our date was a short errand Peter had to run in the village. He kissed me good-bye and skipped out the door. He was as eager to return to me as I was to be with him.

There is something in humility which strangely exalts the heart.

—Saint Augustine

I was upstairs putting some laundry away when I suddenly heard two people talking downstairs. Oh, no, I thought, the spell is broken. Peter was talking to a complete stranger, an architect, who had bumped into him on the street and had wanted to know how he could get a copy of one of Peter's books. Peter had invited him inside.

I was dismayed. My husband, the quintessential gentleman, was also not one to pass up an opportunity to display one of his books. He graced his guest with a signed copy of his book, *Rascals: The Selling of the Legal Profession,* about a new breed of attorneys more interested in taking money from the client than serving the public interest. He also went so far as to invite his admirer to sit down by the fire while he autographed the book. Who wouldn't have taken up Peter's offer to come in from the chill outside?

> *Learning is not child's play; we cannot learn without pain.*
>
> *—Aristotle*

I listened in disbelief. When I called to Peter to come upstairs, he cheerfully replied, "I'm busy, darling. I'm with a friend." Within seconds my mood swung from rapture to the opposite end of the spectrum, disappointment. I had assumed Peter was feeling trapped by the stranger and my interruption would enable him to go gracefully and say good-bye. But I was the one who was trapped, not Peter. This stranger was occupying the energy and the atmosphere Peter and I had intended to enjoy privately. My lover temporarily became a stranger to me. When Peter finally came up to the bedroom, he saw immediately how insensitive he'd been. He knew there was nothing he could say to excuse his thoughtlessness.

I could have lost my temper and asked, "Are you crazy? Don't you understand anything about passion?" Instead, I realized this was an excellent time to raise Peter's consciousness. I talked to him about the art of "no." I suggested he keep his date with me rather than with someone he met in a random encounter in the village. I also explained that it's difficult to ask for tenderness and love. I could see I was getting through to him.

When we've let each other know where we're vulnerable, the lines of communication remain vibrant. Peter personally hadn't hurt me; his evident actions had. By not feeling directly accused, Peter was open to seeing what he had done; he saw how his unwitting episode of carelessness could have had a negative effect on the person he most loves.

Our intense initial conversation began to flow into soothing words that smoothed things over, moving toward the intimacy we had felt before the appearance of the architect. When we married, Peter and I made a pledge never to go to bed feeling separated. Better to stay up half the night unraveling our disagreements than to turn our backs on each other. What a waste to have all that powerful energy dissipate into sadness when it could be redirected into the happiness of love. We not only kiss good night and exchange private words of love, we begin our sleep and dream state holding hands and touching toes.

There in the living room that night, sitting in front of the fire, we slowly moved our energy toward reconciliation. We played a favorite David Lang tape, *Beloved.* As we listened to "Return to the Heart," "First Light," "Courage of the Wind," "Angel of Hope," "Reveries," we

Nine times in ten the heart governs understanding.

—*Lord Chesterfield*

became emotionally attuned and connected. We communicated affectionately, and therefore, effectively. And reconciliation provided an opportunity to appreciate our powerful, poignant hold on each other. We melted back together in tenderness, warmth, and affection. As I lay on my tummy on an antique quilt, I relaxed, gazing into the fire, and Peter rubbed my back as a healer. All the blocked energy became redirected, rechanneled into love.

Letting go of tension frees up loving energy. When you stop a confrontation, you find you have more power to increase your love than you ever thought possible. To his credit, Peter has a great ability to humble himself and apologize. When he kisses to make up, I melt. Ironically, we might have hugged more tenderly and with more heartfelt understanding that night than had we not faced this impasse together. There, with the fire and candles flickering to remind us of the fire of our love, we were one, whole and united. I felt the blessed reciprocity of our affection. Every conflict in love, however severe, is an opportunity to grow closer, offering us new opportunities to discover our true love. What a mysterious—and exciting—process living in love is.

Faith is the bird that feels the light and sings while the dawn is still dark.

—*Rabindranath Tagore*

The Defining Moments of Love

A friend told me recently that all intimate relationships, all our love of others, is a series of defining moments. Each fresh moment of awareness is a way for us to become more conscious, more in tune with ourselves, with each other and the space between us. We experience in our lives incidents that become watersheds, testing our true expansiveness in loving. These transcendent, defining moments allow us to see our lives more clearly than at any other time. I lived through such a defining experience with Peter. This trauma taught me the true depths of my feelings for Peter and the mettle of my desire to live as a loving human being.

My relationship with Peter was severely tried during the first years of our marriage when his teenage son was acting out his anguish over his mother's long-term, irreversible coma. These difficulties reached a climactic point one Sunday night when Peter and I returned after a weekend spent visiting a dying friend to discover that our apartment had been relentlessly trashed. More than fifty wild teenagers had come to an "open house" weekend, slept in all the beds, drunk all the wine, beer, and liquor, broken antiques, porcelain, and other things, thrown up on floors, and purloined everything they could manage to carry with them, including personal treasures, destroying, in effect, the home we had been building together. Our private lives had been cruelly violated. Peter's young son was supposed to be spending the weekend away with older siblings, but he had lied to them and us about his plans, and instead threw a big party, inviting a slew of friends and acquaintances, that disintegrated and exploded to such an extent that our neighbors, frightened by the endless noisy melee, had called the police.

No pleasure is fully delightsome without communication.

—*Michel de Montaigne*

When Peter and I entered the building, Paul, the doorman, looked troubled and nervous. Peter grabbed me and gave me a bear hug and a tender kiss as he usually does before turning the key to the locked apartment. When we entered the front hall, the floor was so filthy and sticky from spilled alcohol, food, and broken glass that my shoes stuck to the wood. The stench of vomit made me feel faint. We found Peter's son in the kitchen, standing with a broom and garbage bag, sweeping up the debris, including fragments of cut crystal glasses and treasured antique dishes.

My open heart shriveled. Having spent the weekend in the company of a frail, ill friend, I felt especially vulnerable. I longed to return to our cozy apartment, to make pea soup and ham sandwiches, to be with the girls, who had spent the weekend with friends.

When you have made your point, sit down.

—Peter Megargee Brown

My Zen calm evaporated and I went crazy, throwing myself into a rage I can still recall vividly, many years later. I felt completely out of control for the first time in my life. I was over the edge. The only thing I could think of doing was to remove myself from the situation. I asked Peter to come to the bedroom where I hugged him and sobbed my hollow heart out. I felt such outrage toward this teenage child I could barely contain myself. I arranged for the girls to come home from their weekend sleepover, and we called the police. For this youthful invasion, Peter felt this was appropriate. We both felt it would take someone with authority to scare the child into consciousness of what he had done. My screaming would clearly not be heard by him.

To love is an expression of one's power to love.

—Erich Fromm

But worse, I felt that I couldn't take the family situation any longer. At one point that evening I pulled out my suitcases and began packing. I wanted a home for my young daughters, not hell on earth. I realized that no matter how much I loved Peter, I was in over my head. I decided I'd take the girls to a hotel where we could be calm and leave Peter to take care of his youngest son. The sheer chaos and shocking reality of what had happened forced me to put a sharp focus on what I wanted. The central reason Peter and I had married each other was to join our children and be a warm, loving family. This was bedlam.

I felt horrible; horrible for Peter's son, who was troubled, horrible for Peter, whose beloved child had caused him so much pain, horrible for myself to have been reduced to such feelings toward a child, and horrible that I felt my only choice was to leave. As I packed, Peter began to cry, pleading with me not to leave. "Alexandra, you knew that we'd face problems with our children; their sheer number increases the odds of conflict. We've discussed this possibility before and we promised each other we would stick together no matter what. You promised we'd always find a way of working things out. If you leave me now you'll break my heart. I love you. I'm just as upset as you are. What has happened is unacceptable. I will forgive my son but I will never forget what he has done. I would do anything for you but sometimes circumstances are beyond my control to protect you. I'm sorry beyond words. This is a nightmare, but I need you now more than ever. I want you to stay. Please, Alexandra, I love you."

All . . . have their frailties and whoever looks for a friend without imperfections will never find what he seeks. We love ourselves notwithstanding our faults, and we ought to love our friends in like manner.

— Cyrus

I was devastated. I was pulled in two different directions: between self-preservation and reaching out to Peter. I kept thinking that I needed peace to raise my two girls. Yet when I turned to Peter and looked into his eyes, I knew I couldn't leave. I wanted to be with Peter, my other half, to enjoy a rich, full family life, and to continue this wonderful relationship where we'd already put in so much love and care. Am I getting what I want? What do I want? I felt compelled to ask.

Knowing what you ultimately want from a lifelong loving relationship is different from setting expectations for another human being. It is up to each of us to discover what we want and to do our best to create the circumstances that will supply us with what we need. In the most essential ways, I was getting what I wanted from my marriage to Peter. Because of all the difficulties involved in uniting our large family, I realized this incident was a turning point. I had to think on my feet—amidst a cyclone of dread and horror. I feared this darkness would threaten all my bright hopes. Would I ever be able to have a calm life again? Would the energy between us ever be the same? Was I courageous enough to stay and set limits I could live with?

It takes a great man to make a good listener.

—Arthur Helps

Peter and I hugged, kissed, and wiped each others' tears. We sat down on the love seat in the bedroom to think things through together. With the door locked, my bag packed, we listened to some of the music we love. I could begin to feel the strength I needed to stay. It was Peter who I loved. We would have to find a way to be together no matter what.

The girls returned and we took them to a restaurant where we could regain our composure while Peter's son was sent to his room to think over the incident. I felt joy in seeing them, having always tried to spare them from knowing how agonizing this family situation was for me.

My commitment to stay with Peter that night was a light on my path. Through it I could see how strong I was capable of being for what I believed in. I accepted my limitations in this circumstance. But I felt brave enough to face the challenges brought on by what was, after all, a child crying out for help.

Later on, after considering how to help the boy, we all discussed what was best to do for him. He finally made the choice to go to a fine boarding school in Newport, Rhode Island. After deliberation we agreed to this direction for him. In the end it was the best thing we all could have done for him. He learned and developed. He actually thrived in the school's strongly disciplined, but caring, honorable atmosphere.

We all cope differently with the inevitable blows of life. Is it possible to live in love when there's so much pain under your roof? As you can see from my story, I would answer that with a heartfelt yes. Unless your partner and you are participating in making life miserable, there is hardly any outside problem that cannot be overcome. That isn't to say that finding the solution or living through the trauma is easy, but the strength and love you draw upon to see each other through is profound and life-affirming. Love doesn't get more potent than that.

We pardon to the extent that we love.

—La Rochefoucauld

Emotional Wisdom

Just as the seasons bring new buds that bloom to their peak before they wither and die, we, too, have cycles of regeneration in our lives. John Coburn refers to these as chapters. We all wish we had known beforehand what we know now. I was giving a talk in Lexington, Kentucky, one Saturday afternoon, when a young blond woman came up and asked why I hadn't started writing books earlier. "Ms. Stoddard, your words about the importance of every moment are really speaking directly to me. I thought I was alone in thinking these thoughts about being present, and aware of every little thing being important. It made me feel odd. Now I feel I'm understood and somehow I feel I can get going and be myself." I smiled and said, "We all feel these stirrings of our own deeper resources, but it takes time to understand ourselves and each other. I wish I'd known when I was younger what I now know about human behavior and frailty, but whether we like it or not, we must experience a whole lot of living before we can thread the connections together in our soul, brain, and in our total awareness."

One joy scatters a hundred griefs.

—*Chinese proverb*

Life is a seamless process and we can't skip steps. We will never appreciate what happens in chapter two if we haven't read or lived chapter one. How wonderful to be able to *learn* from experience rather than repeat our own foibles. Our real concern should not be that we have to go through pain to learn about true joy, but that we might fail to learn at all and remain stuck in melancholy and depression. We can't live life in reverse. If we learn about the process of vital living, we learn the secret to living in love. If we're paying attention, each experience has a way of informing us and preparing us for the next step.

Only the man of understanding really understands.

—*Carl Jung*

We'll never be able to control everything exactly to our liking, just as we can't control the weather. Marriage is, to a degree, a leap of faith. You never know what the future may bring. If we turn love into an inflexible contract, where each of us is assigned to do specific things in certain ways, we limit the infinite possibilities love holds for us if we are able to make our love unconditional. Love must be flexible, alive, spirited—serendipitous.

"Are you getting what you wanted?" Most of us want to appreciate life's blessings, while sharing and deepening our lives with loving people. We are continuously called to elevate ourselves with positive loving energy. By understanding how emotional and spiritual forces come into play in our difficulties, and what skills we can use to turn these situations into opportunities for deepening our bond, we can, with the gift of grace and the divine force of love, work miracles. When we recognize that our deepest need is to love—that all of us want this love—we should do everything we can simply to move along our path.

> *Love can be afraid of nothing.*
>
> —*Seneca*

The more whole and complete I am, the more unity I feel with others. Examine yourself, and see where your own greatness lies, and challenge yourself to use your varied gifts. We start where we are in our own lives. What do you love to do to express your own creativity? What brings you greatest joy?

> *Every individual nature has its own beauty.*
>
> —*Emerson*

By caring about things of substance, about what really matters, you'll resolve situations and know that your power comes from within. Your contentment lies here, and you can then use love as your wings.

Love is always personal. Erich Fromm writes, "There is only one proof for the presence of love: the depth of the relationship, and the aliveness and strength in each person concerned; this is the fruit by which love is recognized." Whatever is love is true. "If two people who have been strangers, as all of us are," Fromm believed, "suddenly let the wall between them break down, and feel close, feel one, this moment of oneness is one of the most exhilarating, most exciting experiences in life." I believe this moment of oneness is the moment you enter into the aura of living in love.

The human body experiences a powerful gravitational pull in the direction of hope.

—*Norman Cousins*

If we can get along with our self, *being* in this loving consciousness as our basic attitude and personal perspective, uniting with another soul will empower and enlarge both of us. Peter and I came together in this open, loving spirit. I look up to him with admiration and respect and have since the day we met. The great privilege for me is to honor him in all ways at all times. Peter, in turn, looks up to me, esteems me, is proud of me, and believes in my character and courage. We live in the awareness that, as the marriage vows informed us, "Marriage is for your mutual joy."

The coach of the Scottish runner in the movie *Chariots of Fire* encouraged him after his rival made him fall in a crucial race, saying, "*Get up, lad. Get up.*" Love requires support and concentration, an active energy of the soul, a personal vision and commitment, the belief in elation within you. If you're brave and tough, love will point the way. Challenge your inner resources. Look at all people and know the individual self of another is you, universally. Understand yourself, and you understand me. Love yourself, and you will be loving me.

Try, try again.

—*William Edward Hickson*

The thirteenth-century German mystical theologian, Meister Eckehart, wrote of this, saying, "If you love yourself, you love everybody else as you do yourself. As long as you love another person less than yourself, you will not really succeed in loving yourself, but if you love all alike, including yourself, you will love them as one person." When you arrive at this awareness of living in loving oneness, you have found your true self and you are on your path. The constant challenge is to increase your focus and attention during the tough times, to be strong when there is a conflict, not just when there's harmony. In joy and sadness love is there, and is the way to heal, to grow, and to become.

Real maturity is the ability to imagine the humanity of every person as fully as you believe in your own humanity.

— Tobias Wolff

"Are you getting what you wanted?" What we all want is to grow more loving. This does not mean fulfilling each other's immediate needs more effectively, but entwining each other's souls and together building a bridge to divinity, ascending to a more luminous consciousness. Love unites us. The ancient Chinese sage Chuang-tzu teaches, "That which is one is one. That which is not one, is also one." We are all connected, one to another. We don't love one other person, our essential love is universal, and the person we want to become, committed to in love, can be beautifully nourished and cared for by our self, and our love. This is the only way to be true, and the only way to live in love.

4.

Creating a Loving Atmosphere

I want to paint the air which surrounds the bridge, the house, the boat: the beauty of the air in which these objects are located. . . .

— CLAUDE MONET

Tending to Love

At heart I've always been a gardener. Peter and I love to work the soil and watch things grow by our hands and the seed. We have spent endless hours of delight in our Zen garden. We choose plants and seeds, learn their properties, and tend them with loving energy. We try never to take anything for granted. If we stop caring for our garden it will perish. The soil will not always be fertile and the sky will not consistently provide water. Neither will the garden always respond to our careful ministrations. Still, we know that through honest, serious effort, with patience, energy, enthusiasm, and a respect for the inner workings of nature, our loving input will always create the possibility for a beautiful blooming spring. If it doesn't, at least we know we have made our best effort— something good always comes of that.

Every spirit builds itself a house, and beyond its house a world, and beyond its world a heaven. Know then that world exists for you.

—Emerson

The nurturing of a garden is similar to the creative act of giving to others. In his thoughtful work, *The Tibetan Book of Living and Dying,* Sogyal Rinpoche focused on our commitment to each other: "Remember, your task is not to convert anyone or anything, but to help that person in front of you get in touch with his or her strength, confidence, and spirituality, whatever that might be." An insight both wise and needed in our world. We take special care not to try and change each other but to show each other support without conditions. For our love to increase, we must care for and nurture all we hold dear with our loving energy and a tender understanding of the souls of those we love. When we direct our loving attention to what is beautiful and true, as we live in love together, we all blossom. If one of us is going through a difficult passage in life, it is essential that we provide a nurturing atmosphere to keep loving energy alive.

Pick today's fruits.

—Horace

There are days when we feel spirited, doing many fulfilling, creative tasks, feeling such a sense of ourselves in what we do that we are in a temporary state of overabundance; "Our cup runneth over." We go out to greet the world and everyone appears receptive. We're complimented on our refreshing expression, engaging smile, our colors, ideas, manner, and performance. When we have these memorable days, the well of life bubbles up and spills over.

I recall one sweet sunny Saturday afternoon when my spirits were soaring but Peter had the flu. He wanted to be left alone. He didn't want to go anywhere or do anything. He didn't even want to eat or play. He wanted me to go away. The sunny day was of no help to him at all, and my cheerfulness about it came across as unctuous. "Leave me alone." I was distressed because I was looking forward to our spending a beautiful day together. Here I was filled with enthusiasm and bursting with romantic energy, and Peter was under a cloud. While he was napping, I decided to spend the afternoon preparing a lavish dinner and quietly puttering around downstairs so I wouldn't disturb him while he rested. Perhaps, by evening, Peter would feel better and we could celebrate, sharing a romantic evening.

Loving energy is never wasted. I delighted in preparing a sumptuous dinner of shrimp and fresh garden fruits and vegetables, thinking good thoughts about Peter's recuperation. I love spending time in the kitchen because it has four windows, all with good views. One overlooks our Zen garden, lush with English ivy climbing up a white trellis. When we had a friend install a mirror behind the latticework in our tiny walled-in backyard, I hadn't envisioned the dancing light from the harbor bouncing back into the kitchen, thrilling me so. Even though we see only a sliver of water from the backyard or out the kitchen window, the pulsating energy and dappling light reflects into the house quite magically because of this hidden mirror on the trellis. I moved around the kitchen that afternoon caught up in a joyful trance.

As the sun set I used the dining room as the backdrop for a landscape of beautiful objects. I selected one of my favorite tablecloths, a bold flower print hand-painted by a friend who is a textile artist.

One must put all the happiness one can into each moment.

—Edith Wharton

The wide blue border is brilliant indigo, a purplish blue shade Peter and I love. I rolled large white, freshly ironed linen dinner napkins in pottery napkin rings decorated with delicate sprigs of flowers in all the colors of the cloth. I placed a blue-and-white hand-blown Venetian glass pitcher from Murano in the center of the table, remembered watching a master glass-blower as he conjured up delicate cones of colored glass, giving shape to his red-hot artistic creation ten years ago when we were on a family vacation in Italy. The girls and I begged Peter, almost on hands and knees, to let us buy this pitcher, even though it meant dragging it around hill towns in a tote bag. I thought about Alexandra and Brooke on that trip, while I filled the pitcher with a boldly colorful bouquet of delphiniums, white lilies, and zinnias. Then I took out our most quietly elegant large dinner plates with striped bands of shades of blue, and selected white salad dishes, each with one iris painted in the center and an apple green border. They looked so pretty on the patterned cloth. What a luxury to have time and peace of mind to arrange beauty.

I selected two kinds of sparkling glasses, one old-fashioned with etching, the other a classic tulip shape, dazzling in the pink light of dusk. I stepped back, realizing the table looked as pretty as an Impressionist still life. I savored time looking in the candle drawer, enjoying all the colors, eventually picking two tall azure beeswax ones, setting them in a pair of polished antique brass candlesticks, placing hurricane globes over them so the wax wouldn't drip on the hand-painted tablecloth in the evening wind. The blue of the candles picked up the colors of the delphiniums and the whole play of color, texture, and light on the table came together, mysteriously beautiful, alive, and sensuous. What a pleasure for me. The evening was truly lovely. I can't remember a more flaming sunset or a more lovely glow in the house.

When you sow love, joy grows.

— German proverb

Peter was still upstairs resting in bed, feeling chilled despite the warm summer air. Should I go upstairs and gently invite him to come to dinner? I wanted him to share the love and joy I was feeling. Instead of being anxious, worrying about him with his flu, I was Zen, remaining in a loving place. If Peter needed to rest, if he didn't feel up to coming downstairs for dinner, that was fine; I might bring dinner upstairs for us. I'd play it by ear. We could sit around the cricket table in the bedroom and dine there. I would blow out the candles on the dining room table and set up a pretty tray. I'd had my pleasure in the day, creating a work of art for us. I was content where I was, even if the evening wouldn't turn out as I'd originally hoped.

I remained in the kitchen peeling some gorgeous sun-ripened tomatoes. From the open window I heard a band warming up. Umpa, umpa. It was Labor Day weekend, and we villagers have a Souza band that plays for us on holidays. The music was an added delight. Everything was very alive for me. As I mused over the wonderful tapestry of life around me, Peter suddenly appeared at the kitchen door smiling his "just for me" smile, double thumbs-up. His hair was freshly washed and combed back and shiny. He looked radiant in his cool blue shirt. "I feel better," he said. Then he told me about his glorious bath and the pink glow in the sky, and the shimmering light from the harbor that was reflected on the walls and ceiling of the bathroom. I was happy for him and glad to hear him say,

Listen. Think first of someone else. Laugh a little. Gladden the heart of another human being. Take pleasure in the beauty and wonder of the earth. Speak your love. Speak it still once again.

—*Anonymous*

"The table looks magnificent, darling. It looks as though we're in for a feast."

As we sat at the table enjoying our private celebration, I looked at Peter sitting across from me and my heart was flooded with tenderness and joy. The candles melted to the quick as we lingered at the dining room table until after eleven o'clock, amusing ourselves with old stories and enjoying the music next door. If you want to live in love you can't turn on your affection when it's convenient, but you seize the reality of the present as an opportunity to live lovingly, now. We may not be responsible for each other's happiness, but we are each responsible for creating the happiness we seek.

Achieving Perpetual Sunlight

I recall how last summer, one dank, drizzly day lifted to a dazzling afternoon and my spirits began to fly. The weather has a powerful effect on our outlook. Researchers have discovered a mood disorder, the inability to feel happiness that results from a lack of natural light, particularly problematic during winter months, when light is short. This illness, called Seasonal Affective Disorder (S.A.D.), now, I'm told, can be treated with special lights. We thrive on light just as nature does because it is our main source of energy.

As bees gather honey, so we collect what is sweetest out of all things and build.

—*Rainer Maria Rilke*

But even when the weather is bad we can listen to classical music, light the lights, clean out a closet or organize the kitchen drawers, and putter around the house. A friend looked out of the window in her office when there was a storm. "Sandie," she told me, "aren't we lucky we love our work? Today, we're not torn by not being able to play outside."

Empathy and Emotional Generosity

When you live in love you can delve into a deeper reservoir of emotional possibility. Your capacity to be understanding can soar. I love knowing that Peter and everyone I love feels I am there for them 100%; they can depend on me to always try my best to put myself in their shoes. Through the pure energy of love we can become an instrument for love feeling the dynamic force embracing the sacredness of each other's destinies, and finding the strength to understand and to give of ourselves.

Light is the atmosphere of love. Love is the atmosphere of light.

—Peter Megargee Brown

Recognizing our spouse as a separate being with an individual personality, complex feelings, different beliefs and background, shows respect and creates a place for empathy to grow. To be empathetic we must be able to put ourselves in another person's situation regardless of how we feel.

When Peter prepares for a difficult legal case I answer the telephone for him and clear the calendar so he is free to study. During these periods we limit who is invited to the apartment or cottage so he has quiet and peace to think through his work. We try to live by the Golden Rule. If I were responsible for going to court to defend a client, I'd want to be prepared. I take Peter's work seriously and identify with his needs even though they are different from mine.

When you love someone you develop an objectivity, because you are in tune with their feelings and tend to be less influenced by emotions or personal prejudices. You put the other person's needs above your own desires. You stand back and try to look at the larger picture. This never feels burdensome, but is a time of great intimacy. One evening Peter announced he had invited a friend to have tea in the apartment the following day when I was struggling to meet a deadline. I had to explain to Peter how I wanted to be alone and sit still in the apartment in order to concentrate on my work. When Peter saw the situation through my perspective, he immediately understood, and rather than having his friend come to the apartment that afternoon, he met him at a nearby hotel tearoom. Being able to communicate honestly opens us up to greater empathy.

Feel: touch, taste, smell, hear, see, and intuit directly. Experience love concretely—love a tree, a sunset, a cloud, a bee buzzing, a child singing.

Empathy comes naturally to committed, mature, loving people. When you grow to understand that the people you love are one with you, how you would feel in their situation is similar to how the loved person is feeling. Why would I deliberately try to hurt you if you and I are one? Empathy requires sensitivity. Peter and I are sufficiently sensitive to know how our actions make each other feel. Neither of us enjoys being criticized. We know right from wrong, not wanting to be told what to do or how to act or think. When our son or daughter comes home from school in tears because another child has said something mean and hurtful, we intuitively feel the weight of our child's sorrow. Immediately, we want to rush to their side and take the rejection and hurt away with our love. We feel our love as a powerful ameliorative force.

Giving generously to anyone in need always increases your love potential, making you and others feel better. Love keeps us open to the suffering of others. Our empathy extends to our sense of touch, just as a mother's kissing a "boo boo" helps her child. Several months ago I painfully banged my right elbow against the window on a crowded train. The pain was excruciating. I have chronic tennis elbow that sometimes bothers me when I write and I usually sit in an aisle seat to give that elbow freedom. But rather than standing on this particular ride, I took the only available seat, next to the window. Peter turned pale when he saw my pain, and leaned over and tenderly kissed my elbow. Everyone laughed, but I honestly felt better because of his physical touch. When I'm grieving over the death of a friend I want to be hugged. Shaking hands is fine for some, but I want hugs, especially when I'm hurting.

Feeling what others feel is a natural ability when you live in love. The same love and understanding we give to a child, our spouse, or a close friend can also be beamed to strangers. Think of the outpouring of love and generosity of spirit you feel when you read in the newspaper about some tragic, fatal accident. You pray for the victims and their families, and you may send a check or a sympathy letter. Suffering is central to the human condition, but sages throughout history have tried to illuminate us to only die once, and to be awake to the magical, mysterious force called love. How do we heal ourselves? How do we heal others? Love.

Creating a Loving Space

From the time I was a child first learning the rituals and pleasures of living in an attractive home and appreciating a blooming garden, I have sought to create beautiful spaces for my family and clients. One of the most shortsighted things a person can do is buy a house as an investment to be sold when the real estate market rises. Profit is gained at the expense of creating a home for their family. Continuity and a true spirit of place for future generations is priceless.

When the green woods laugh with the voice of joy . . .

— William Blake

When we create a pure, loving environment, we fill our house with the juicy, generous, aliveness of love, transforming it into a home with soul, filled with sentimental objects of our affection.

All the pretty objects we've gathered over the years, from the delicate embroidered white square pillow shams with scalloped borders Peter and I bought in Madeira, Portugal, to the antique enamel pillboxes we collect, fill our home with warmth, beauty, and a tangible love experienced through the senses. Looking around our home at the paintings and pottery we love, reacquainting myself with them, recalling their provenance, I welcome the magic they cast on my soul. We make our home as beautiful as we can because it is an outward expression of our love of life.

When we're sensitive to the way certain spaces make us feel, we fill our home with love and beauty, and grace appears. Home should always be a comfortable place where we can be totally ourselves. Sometimes that means home is not always orderly. When we've spent time at home reading, working, doing projects, enjoying crafts, looking through old things, rooms gradually become crowded with signs of our interests. Rather than worry about the accumulation, Peter and I prefer to defer the tidying up to a later time, after we've completed our various pursuits. One morning, I went downstairs to get a dictionary from the round table in the living room. I found quite a sight. Yesterday's newspaper was spread out on the floor, there were six books on the seat of one chair, as well as several others strewn on the round upholstered ottoman. In front of the fireplace, on a low square fruitwood table, was a tea tray with a plate of ginger-snaps, left over from the afternoon before.

Love and light cannot be hid.

—*James Kelly*

This place is *real*. People *live* here. Interior decorators try to create the "lived-in look," not always understanding the truth about the way people really live. You have to live fully every moment, not neatening up while you're in the midst of enjoying yourself.

Peter and I don't mind when the house looks lived in because we understand that when you're engaged in real living, the stuff of life is evident. I like getting down to work and don't mind becoming soiled. Everything I like to do, including read-ing, writing, gardening, decorating, painting, and cooking is real, alive, and requires getting your hands, as well as your rooms, dirty. But there's order to the seemingly chaotic space because we both need to have our things around to inspire, stimulate, delight, and add convenience. Our end tables may look appalling, but we care about the papers, clippings, maga-zines, and books they hold. We eat and drink in all our rooms and feel comfortable spreading out projects with abandon.

Peter told me about one evening when he was ten and his father woke him up and exclaimed, "How could you go to sleep without closing your closet door? I've never seen a messier room. It looks as if a cyclone struck it." His father then com-plained to his mother, "Peter never has learned to put anything back." When I was growing up I was usually dirty because I was having fun, lost in my own thoughts, exploring nature, digging in the soil, climbing trees. I smelled earthy from the horse barn or my garden. Having clean fingernails was not just unimportant, it was impossible because the soil actually stained my fingers. Once when my mother complained about my appearance to my godmother, Mitzi Christian, she said, "Sandie is always dirty. Her blouse is never tucked in. She looks like a ragamuffin." Mitzi responded, "Barbara, Sandie is a gardener. Have you ever seen a gardener who was worth anything who had clean fingernails? You can't wear white gloves when you garden. Sandie can wear them afterwards, to hide her dirty nails if you like, but remember what's more important."

Being best, brightest and most rational does not guarantee either wisdom or virtue. Empathy is necessary too.

— Claudia Koonz

Because Peter and I were forbidden to be messy growing up, it's especially enjoyable to be able to do what feels right as we go along without worrying about tidiness. There are books everywhere, as well as mail and notes, but we know where everything is and appreciate the luxury of not having to impress or satisfy anyone with neatness. We'd rather be involved in a lot of interesting pursuits than feel any need to be tidy. Living in love is a process of discovering what gives life value. An unmade bed could be a loving bed.

The more lovingly you place each object, the more inviting the spaces will feel. You logically place chairs where people will feel most comfortable sitting, where you'd want to sit, relax, feel at ease. You intuitively know always to arrange seating where people can share a good view and good conversation, even if this means looking into another attractive, colorful room.

Peter's desk in the apartment is in the far left corner of the living room facing out into the room so he can take in all the glorious colors, textures, and art as well as light. He sees through the living room into the long hall, always able to feast his eyes on a favorite painting, and beyond the hall into the kitchen, where he looks at a ficus tree beside a large picture window, suggesting air, space, light, and beauty in a relatively small urban space.

When inanimate objects are loved, appreciated, brought to life, they bring joy to everyone. When I look around our home I imagine the delight our children, grandchildren, and friends enjoy when they walk in and are greeted by so many personally meaningful things, so many treasures we've selected together on family trips. The children love the quilt collection, the Roger Mühl paintings, and the Anne Gordon porcelains, and they always seem to be happy to know there will be fresh flowers in their rooms. The pastel-colored candies in cotton candy–colored bowls surprise them with a sweet delight.

Real generosity is doing something nice for someone who'll never find out.

—*Frank A. Clark*

In our cottage I placed the sofa so family and friends can enjoy the light from the west windows, as well as see the boats come and go from the harbor. (Someone once asked me what my favorite window is in all the houses I've decorated. I pointed to a simple, unadorned window in our bedroom where I sit at a pine table, looking down at the water.) I put the upholstered swivel chairs facing the sofa so the light from the windows is behind us while we enjoy reading. We can swing around, watching the spectacular sunsets in reverie. This seating arrangement is ideal for conversation as well as pleasant contemplation. Our large round chintz ottoman is a shared footrest where we can touch toes or place books and newspapers, or where a grandchild can sit.

One of the joys of home is preparing a delicious meal together, spending hours enjoying the food as well as the companionship in a charming ambiance with candles and music. Dishes in the sink are a witness to a love of living. If we can't enjoy this homey scene in the kitchen, a happy still life of a *real* home, we're not truly living in love. We have a large Mühl painting in the kitchen of our cottage of a table after a luncheon. (Roger Mühl paints scenes of the everyday—the table, the food, the wine. He told me recently why he usually has a window or a door in his paintings: "It allows the imagination to go inside or out, as well as the fantasies.") In the painting, red wine is left in the glass, fruit on the plate, bread crumbs and wrinkled napkins on the table, speaking of the joy of domestic life.

One kind word can warm three winter months.

—Japanese saying

Hanging around home is heavenly. Even if the outside world is troubled with hostility and complaints, home can be a private sanctuary. I love to spend unscheduled time at home with Peter, feeling the luxury of our intimacy. We greet each moment of life with a greater sense of ease because our loving home renews us, reverberates with our love, resounding with our spirit. You feel home's imprint wherever you are, knowing it is there, waiting for you.

I recall one wonderful weekend when I was tired and sick with bronchitis. I needed to rest, to be calm in a loving atmosphere in order to recuperate naturally. Peter and I retreated to our cottage in Stonington. During the three days and nights of our escape we sat by warm fires, reading, talking, listening to music, and holding hands. One evening we were enraptured as we dined on smoked salmon, some blue cheese, and a crust of freshly baked, and still warm, bread purchased at a new bakery a few hundred yards from our house.

After dinner we lingered over a pot of chamomile tea at the kitchen table. Whenever we're in the cottage we feel caressed by a loving presence. We've put so much affection and attention into all the details, the cottage always seems to radiate love

Love spreads a feeling of sanctity in the atmosphere, sweetening the air.

back to us. Love echoes. That night, it felt as if everything we'd put into our home all these years was evident in the sweet feelings of contentment. Everything seemed to be gathered together in this moment, expanding to enchantment, where we experienced such thanksgiving. We felt the blessings of this cottage, how it bestows us, our family, and friends with loving radiance, almost as though the walls were able to move toward us and tenderly hug us. We could feel ourselves held here, at home, in love's timeless embrace. My recovery was rapid, thank goodness. Our cottage is our utopia, modest, honest and genuine.

With varying degrees of success, I've attempted to awaken in others an enthusiasm for light, clear, fresh garden colors. This has not always been easy, especially when people wanted to create "sophisticated" spaces, often devoid of fresh colors because brightly colored rooms are generally considered naive and even childish, more suitable for a nursery or playroom. I want people to experience inside their homes enlargement and awe at the sheer wonder and harmony of nature's lush beauty.

Can we be enchanted with our immediate surroundings, so enraptured that our mood, attitude, and spirit are transformed?

Why do we feel such a sense of utter sweetness when we are outside in the sunshine, among growing, living colors and forms? What lessons do we learn that we can bring home from a garden in bloom? Is there a connection between this cyclical, fleeting organic beauty, light, and atmosphere of nature that we can create inside where we live? There is something magical about a white cotton curtain blowing in an open window as though frolicking with the sunshine.

If we're willing to open our hearts to our essential feelings, we want the spaces where we live and love to express our own growth, our own flowering and fragility as human beings. Loving people have the capacity to create a loving atmosphere wherever they live. Rooms can be gardens, alive, blossoming, engaging all the senses with private pleasures and treasures that stimulate both our sense of aesthetics and our intellect. We can create loving places where we, and others, are emotionally comfortable as well as spiritually nourished.

A loving person lives in a loving world. . . . Everyone you meet is your mirror.

—*Ken Keyes, Jr.*

Choosing furniture and objects randomly, placing things according to a floor plan, keeping the space neat and tidy, lights out, curtains drawn, is not creating a loving atmosphere. (I didn't become an interior designer because I'm particularly attached to furniture, although after almost four decades of study, I've deepened my appreciation for a wide range of decorative arts, especially antique furniture. But a baby crawling on the floor will always fill my heart with more affection than the most exquisite quality table or chair.)

Have you ever entered someone's home and immediately felt the warmth of their personality, even when they're not there? I certainly have, but I've also been in thousands of spaces where I *feel* the dis-comfort of the owner as soon as I walk through the front door. I often get the feeling they are more concerned with maintaining a picture-perfect, dust-free envi-ronment than actually enjoying their homes. Their rooms may be physically luxurious, filled with museum pieces of furniture and priceless artwork, but they lack warmth, appearing to be frozen, sus-pended from growth and development. Some houses never have an open window.

> *Be not long away from home.*
>
> —*Homer*

It's not how much time you spend cleaning a room that makes it absorb your energy and infused with your spirit. We must spend time *loving* in our personal spaces, awakening our rooms to a vibrancy, a sense of breathing, a refreshing newness that merges us with our physical surroundings. Any room you don't use for your per-sonal pursuits of pleasure, where you don't go alone, where you don't eat and drink, dance, laugh, put your feet up, lean back in a chair, light a fire or candles, sing and lose track of time, will not be a happy space.

We don't escape to a Caribbean island with our love to get stuck in a shelter with no electricity because of Hurricane Luis—if we can help it. We flee to a romantic island to enjoy the sun, the water, and the joy of nature's fleeting impressions, and capture, in an instant, a sense of the supernatural. We seek freshness, sweet-smelling air, warmth and tranquility, so we are more open and responsive to appreciate all the other joyous wonders of life.

When I was on *The Oprah Winfrey Show* in November 1995, the segment was entitled "What Your House Says About You." At one point Oprah asked her audience, "Should we do away with living rooms?" I then asked, "How many of you were in your living rooms this morning?" Oprah went up to one woman who was enthusiastically waving her hand. I inquired, "What were you doing in your living room?" Sadly, but not surprisingly, her answer was, "Cleaning." I laughed and said, "Oh, no." I have no doubt many women are cleaning women in their own living rooms, never fully understanding that being clean doesn't make a space sing. It's similar to going to church without lighting a candle, or singing a hymn, or gazing at the light patterns on the wall from the sun beaming through the stained glass, or reading a psalm, or saying a prayer, or just being present to experience the beauty of the flowers, the music, and the ritual.

The surroundings householders crave are glorified autobiographies.

— *T. H. Robsjohn-Gibbings*

The least understood room in most people's lives is the living room. It is usually the most uptight, outer-directed room, misnamed because in so many houses no real daily living takes place there. If we're aware of all the vital energy we can generate when we're free to express our true nature, why, do you think, we get so stuck, in the mood and attitude of this one room? Thousands of people confess to me their insecurities about this room. Oprah's question is a good one. Should we do away with living rooms? Should we change the name to *loving* room? Maybe if we associated this room with loving in this literal way, we would spend more time there, creating good karma. Obviously we'll have to keep this notion to ourselves for fear of people thinking we're insane. But if we concentrate on unfolding our personality and spirit into the living or *loving* room just as we do our bedroom or kitchen, we will feel drawn to spend happy hours there every day. I like to think of our living room as a garden. What does yours look like? How have you expressed your passion in this space so the energy vibrates refreshingly as you reach out in loving ways to yourself and others? You may not have a fireplace in this room, but, as van Gogh said, we can have the flame in our soul.

One of my favorite living rooms was in a farmhouse in Northampton, Massachusetts, where my art teacher Phyl Gardner lived with her husband, Jimmy, and a friend when I was at boarding school in Northampton. Phyl was an artist and her living room was her studio.

Beauty inspires your love for living.

We felt her appreciation for the beauty of the old rambling house, the huge windows opening up to giant oak trees, the comfort and warmth of the atmosphere drawing us together mystically. I loathed the hot milk that accompanied the lemon cookies at bedtime, but the kiss in bed was and remains endearing. The love there at the Gardner farm was so powerfully felt, I think about this ritual often, wondering if Phyl and Jimmy helped me to feel the way I do about ritualizing my life. Every act was kind, every gesture was sweet.

The purest and most thoughtful minds are those which love color the most.

—John Ruskin

While a chicken was roasting in the oven, often we'd look at slides taken from the previous summer's trip to Africa. Jimmy taught architecture and Phyl art, and for three months every summer they traveled to different parts of the world, to sketch, take notes and photographs, and get back in touch with their creative urges. If the urge struck Phyl, she'd sketch a pedestal table with trailing English ivy. There were books everywhere. Phyl taught me the joys of reading dozens of books at once. My little room off the kitchen turned into a lending library. There was no rigid schedule, everything was enjoyed naturally, spontaneously, and it was here where, for the first time in the fifteen years I'd been alive, I felt no tension at all between the occupants of a house. Jimmy and Phyl's love for each other was spirited and because they didn't have any children of their own, they opened their hearts and home to their students. We were an extended family, experiencing the enthusiasm and joy of a loving, creative, happy couple.

Art is an external expression of our inner world.

— William Spear

Relaxed would be too mild a word to describe the atmosphere at the farm. Here I became a student of ease. I was an uptight, preppy teenager from a suburb in Connecticut, fortunate enough to study art and art appreciation from an eccentric English lady. I adored her completely. It was weekends at their farm in the country where I felt the freedom and gaiety missing in so many people's lives back home. The blue seltzer bottle was her friend. She'd squirt it into her Scotch on the rocks, mist and water her plants with it and, when the spirit moved her, she'd spray Jimmy or me or a history professor from Smith College. Every time she got near her blue bottle she'd break out into an infectious giggle. This loving room was lived in, and people's pleasure and sense of play was the focus, not worrying about the furniture. If a lamp broke in these running-around times, the laughter and fun were worth the fall. "I never liked that ugly lamp. Good. Now I don't have to look at it anymore."

Many of my friends tell me they are in "house love." While they may or may not be "in love" with another person, they have such angelic positive feelings about their physical surroundings, they feel exuberant and content. Both Alexandra and Brooke are full of this passion for their living, truly loving spaces.

One of my favorite loving rooms is our daughter Brooke's small but all-encompassing space. Size is not significant when we go about creating a loving atmosphere. Perhaps small *is* beautiful. When people have too much space, the living room becomes extraneous, and is not real. When you live in the center of your space, your vibrancy builds, and the vibrations are charged with you. Brooke lives in her loving space, and her campaign daybed is a sofa where she sleeps. The fifteen-dollar art deco coffee table that she found at a flea market in Chatham, New York, on a Sunday afternoon is stunning. Everything in her loving space is thoughtfully placed and beautiful. She's prepared her space as an artist sketches out a canvas, outlining the colors and beauty. Because Brooke lives in her loving room, it is not merely stylish, it is electric.

Our older daughter, Alexandra, who lives in a garden apartment in Georgetown, feels the same way about her space as her sister. She believes you have to prepare your own atmosphere for love before you're able to connect in a loving way to

> *Love of beauty and the desire to create it is a primal instinct in man.*
>
> —*Eleanor McMillen Brown*

others. One evening a coworker helped Alexandra deliver an antique wicker love seat for her garden room, a space already filled with her loving energy. After the sofa was put in place, the atmosphere was further charged with good feelings, setting the stage for the two to fall in love. Is this a love story or real life? We have to take charge and create our own atmosphere before we can join lovingly with others.

In Alexandra's apartment, you have to pass through the garden room into a kitchen before you reach the living room. Once there, you feel you're in the heart and soul of an intimate atmosphere. Alexandra lives here and the room is energetic, serene, regal, and stylish. She loves her personal space so much, it exudes her enthusiasm. On an antique pine trunk she uses as a coffee table, she has a green glass vase that looks as though it were excavated from Pompeii. One of her favorite flowers is pale purple gladiola, and she buys five tall stems for five dollars, lasting approximately a week. (Most interior designers loathe gladiolas but I, like Alexandra, love them.) The power of these five stems of purple blossoms in the green vase is glorious, and they add significantly to the spirit of place. Alexandra *loves* her home, as Brooke loves hers. You feel this when you're present in their cozy apartments.

Everyone is touched by the way these spaces feel. I believe money and space limitations are not as significant as how we kiss the space with our love. Alexandra's two cats, Clayborn and Lesieur, entertain us while she plays music to celebrate the visit. Brooke floats flowers and candles in a hand-blown bowl on the bottom tier of her coffee table, reflecting light and the mood of ceremony.

The more things you love, the more you are interested in, the more you enjoy.

—*Ethel Barrymore*

When you think about creating a loving atmosphere for yourself, your love, and your family, fantasize about the happiest childhood memories of the nursery, the playroom, the playground, the park, the garden, the lake, the seaside, and the boat. Recall the picnics, the birthday parties, and the family vacations. Remember the sunrises, and sunsets, and the light gleaming through tall trees in the forest. The playful, youthful, candy colors are still the most joyful, so never grow up if it means living a duller life.

Colors and patterns have deep emotional resonance for both Peter and me. Whenever Peter and I travel and enjoy a memorable meal in a romantic restaurant, we ask if we can buy a colorful tablecloth or napkin to bring home so we'll be able to keep that experience alive. Peter loves flowers as much as I do and adores arranging them. Take a man to a flower market and let him run loose and you'll experience the abundant joy color brings. Peter loved the idea of our changing the yellow New York living room to a soft peony pink.

Living in love creates domestic arts where everything is an expression of your appreciation of life's beauty.

Rooms that feel right to us, that are emotionally charged with loving, spirited energy are fresh, and clear and brightly colored. Love is sunny, not dusty. Interior design, in essence, in order to be real, meaningful, and magical, must tune your physical environment to your inner being.

A loving atmosphere should contain a rainbow of favorite colors, in such a wide range you are continuously stimulated by the harmony and breadth of experience.

I love everything that is beautiful, no matter whether it is fresh or foul. My loves are passionate and legion.

—Rose Cummings

Our rooms are living organisms. The atmosphere we create is telling. Everything, each object, the art, the colors, the light, the textures, the shine and sheen, all tell a private story. Home is a sanctuary for those who believe we can grow spiritually right in our own soil, when we are alone, and when we share our spirit with others.

Love is a blueprint for living. Every thought we have resonates; there are recognizable wavelengths in the air, just as with colors. We are all leaflike in our sensitivity, needing sunlight in the atmosphere to flourish. Our human energy has the transcendental power to turn a plain room into an exalted love nest filled with light, to turn an ordinary meal into nourishment for our mind, body, and soul, making it a living celebratory banquet in honor of the gift of life. The energy we put into the spaces where we live and love elevates the ordinary to the extraordinary.

Beauty is silent eloquence.

—French proverb

Living spaces should be loving spaces, never restricting, ever expanding, flexible, changing. All our rooms should be *loving* rooms, always receptive, giving, generous-spirited.

Loving Rituals

When Brooke was seven and old enough to buy me a Mother's Day present, sweet William was all she could afford. All these years later, when Mother's Day arrives, Brooke still brings me sweet William, and I burst into tears of sentimentality and accumulated memories. Remembering what pleases loved ones, treasuring the specific things we enjoy doing together, making a deliberate point to celebrate and incorporate these giving, thoughtful gestures as rituals into our lives, transform the common, ordinary, and average times into rare moments of excellence that elate us. These tender, thoughtful rituals, the ceremonies we share together on a regular basis or for special times—whether it's taking a walk in the park every day or once a week, shopping at the farmers' market, preparing a meal together every Thursday, bringing home fresh flowers on certain days, hand washing t¹ e dishes together, or going to a coffee shop to hang out—the joy of being able to anticipate these customary acts, repeated ceremoniously, resonates in our consciousness.

There is an art to creating meaningful rituals in the fabric of your daily life. With practice, patience, and training, we can greatly increase our sense of joy in the moments as they fly by. I deliberately live my life ritualistically. Allowing ample leeway for serendipity, I love the thousands of little ways we can increase our loving energy. Every moment is an opportunity to love. We can tie a bow in a child's hair, set a pretty tea tray, play the piano, or sing a favorite song. The sunsets, the pretty ironed napkin, the light illuminating a white vase of zinnias, a cut

> *In part, art completes what nature cannot elaborate; and in part, it imitates nature.*
>
> —*Aristotle*

crystal stemmed glass for mineral water, some handsome stationery for writing a sweet note, a fountain pen, a desk placed in front of an open window, a ribbon in a hat, and a colorful patterned scarf tied in a bow around my neck all contribute to a joyful atmosphere. I can get excited about the tiniest thing. Show me a blue-and-white-striped paper clip and I'm in heaven. The other day I stared at some yellow tulips in a cobalt-blue pitcher so intensely, my nose must have turned yellow like a buttercup. Who can say this way of living is a waste of time when it produces such inner sweetness?

When we live in a continuous series of rituals, celebrations, and ceremonies, we increase the dignity of our human lives and elevate our spirit to a more divine existence. Why reserve flowers or loving energy for special occasions? If we truly love beauty, not just the concept, and are willing to *experience* it, travel for it, take time to absorb and appreciate it, we become more loving.

Life is painting a picture, not doing a sum.

—*Oliver Wendell Holmes, Jr.*

If we are honest, authentic, true to our higher selves, we will naturally, spontaneously be drawn to create thoughtful rituals in the rhythm of the day. The only way I know to build a better universe is to create a loving atmosphere at home where you feel tranquility, where you're able to enjoy a better life for yourself and loved ones in a serene, gentle environment. When we accomplish this and feel content, wherever we are, we will want to raise each moment into an exalted one, opening up our senses and our heart to appreciation and praise.

To develop in taste, quality, and personality one is obliged to respect the past, accept the present, and look with enthusiasm toward the future.

—*Eleanor McMillen Brown*

Ritualizing moments brings us opportunities to love others without smothering them, give without needing anything in return, and rise to sublime levels of being.

How can I love life more? A cup of coffee in a pretty cup and saucer can have a dessert dish underneath, making it special. A breakfast tray can have one tiny bud vase, a napkin can be slipped into a ring or rolled. Towels can be cheerful pastels, and you can run a bath, laying out a robe and slippers for a loved one. Use a huge dinner plate for a few tomatoes and basil so the chartreuse drops of olive oil can dance against the white porcelain and bring cheer.

Don't wait for someone to do something *for* you. Be the generous giver, because this is the only way to live in love.

Pretend you are a child at play, and your house is the playground. It is your birthday and everyone else's birthday, too. Use confetti soap in your bath and toast your love, even if you're sipping coffee. If you are awake to the magnificence of the moment, it will be your *birth* day because you will be "awake" in a more profound way.

> *Simplicity and sincerity.*
>
> — *Van Day Truax*

Every evening, whether we've been alone or with family and friends, Peter and I always sit privately in our bedroom and talk before we turn out the lights and kiss good night. Just knowing we'll have this time and space alone comforts us, and we may spend minutes or hours in this state of privacy, depending how the spirit moves us.

Peter and I ritualize the littlest occasions. We go together to get the newspaper, to the post office for stamps, to buy groceries, or to the bookstore. We ritualize our common daily acts and it makes us feel good because they're shared. When we ritualize our days with simple activities that satisfy our aesthetic and spiritual needs, as well as our senses, we treat each other to a poignant sense of the continuity of our days together.

> *Share in a love of home.*

Meaningful rituals, attractively planned and prepared, generate love and miraculously can also become one of the powerful ways to get through an uneasy situation. Even having a reception in your home after a funeral service is always colored with the bittersweet joy of being alive and participating fully in all aspects of living. The rituals you share become part of your personal metaphors of love.

An inner light illuminates our home when we fill it with loving rituals. The winter before last Peter and I were snowed in at
our cottage in the largest December storm since 1960. We had
to cancel our trip to New York and had three additional days to
prepare for Alexandra and Brooke arriving for Christmas. We
were inside a dream. Once we knew we were not going to struggle to get to the city, we settled in, sat in front of roaring fires,
watched the storm, and listened to years' worth of accumulated
Christmas tapes. We took out our tree ornaments and gift-
wrapping paper and ribbons. (I store our ornaments in flowered
hat boxes, along with a large ribbon collection.) I'm so passionate about color, wrapping presents is a gift
I give myself. I tend to overdo it with the
French wired silk taffeta plaids so the
recipient can in turn give the colorful ribbons to someone else when they are tied
on other presents, passing on the mystery.

> *Living in love is
> awaking completely
> to our existence here
> and now.*
>
> —*Peter Megargee Brown*

Listening to Handel's *Messiah*—the
sound of angels expanded in dynamic
range—smelling the spicy, pungent aroma
of the fat, full pine tree, placing handmade ornaments on the
branches, all created by children and adults who refuse to grow
up, putting packages under the tree, throwing some cinnamon-
scented pine cones into the fire, along with the skin of a clemen-
tine to explode in the essence of scent, and taste, made me feel
enveloped inside a fantasy world. In this consciousness, every act,
every move, is infused with abiding, eternal love. Mysteriously,
because we were peacefully preparing for loved ones to come,
our loving energy increased with our joyful anticipation.

Our rituals overlap those of our childhood. Peter and I
remember our Christmas stockings abundant with clementines.

Our grandparents had clementines in *their* stockings. So life and love flow seamlessly forward. His mother always bought a wooden crate of this fruit, grown in Spain. Along with new shiny pennies, tubes of toothpaste, and a rare crisp dollar bill, those sweet, orange citrus balls are a symbol of the holidays, together with rainbow ribbon candy as delicate as cones of spun glass from Murano. I can't imagine December without a compote brimming with clementines. This year we placed some English ivy in the hand-blown bowl and let it trail down to the antique fruitwood table, inviting a spontaneous munch. How powerful it is to have symbolic traditions and rituals that we carry out in our own way, bringing our past up front to participate in our current life.

Why is it that all the ornaments on our tree, year after year, usually end up being created by the hands of children and their parents? The more I understand about love's timelessness, the more I'm miraculously drawn to continuity. I'm able to remember making ornaments for our tree as a little girl and that sense of wonder and anticipation never left me. Not long ago, I realized all the joy you can hang on a pine tree in December. The colorful ribbons and buttons, strung together by babes, angels only a few years old, so pure and able. With trust and supervision they were able to participate in the great ceremony with adults. Year after year we remember who made each ornament, and, as we hang it on the tree, we celebrate Megan, Sally, Brenda, Bill, Walter, Sarah, Blair, Julia, Hillary, James, Darcy,

> *Home is the heart of life. . . . Home is where we feel at ease, where we belong, where we can create surroundings that reflect our tastes and pleasures. . . . Making a home is a form of creativity open to everyone.*
>
> — *Terence Conran*

Alexandra, Brooke, Peter, Paul, and Paula. We are part of a process, a river that flows forward. When all generations are invited to jump in, get their feet wet and participate, love is tangible, tender, and sweet.

A refined simplicity—to be simple is to be great.

—Emerson

My passion for ribbons is inherited. One year when I was a little girl, on our onion farm on Compo Parkway in Westport, Connecticut, my parents created a Christmas tree decorated with nothing but clear lights and red velvet bows. The tree was at the far end of the sunken living room, several feet lower than the blue slate floor of the hallway. For a seven-year-old, the sight of this spectacular tree in this grand space as I descended the stairs was awesomely beautiful. Somehow the simplicity of these red velvet bows made a lasting impression. Once our girls no longer brought home decorations they made in school, I provided colorful materials for us and their friends to make ornaments. Why is it that we always find ways to weave into the fabric of our lives all the personally pleasing elements of our past, so the parts become a whole composition of fragments, patches, and snippets of color and energy that reveal us symbolically and spiritually? So many of the sweet blessings made by children and their parents live on and are appreciated as the years advance. Mrs. Brown wisely warned her employees to be careful about what we throw away. I hold these decorations in high esteem, appreciating them as precious gifts of love and affection. Is there anything infused with more loving karma?

Gratitude is a fruit of great cultivation.

—Samuel Johnson

What a fantastic and stunning feast to the senses and spirit. The radiance that emanates from the colorful ribbons and buttons speaks of more than you and me, and has the power to symbolically connect us, wherever we are, and whether we celebrate Christmas or not. The joy of these celebrations reminds us the impact of ritual in our lives and how everything can become symbolic. It is the memory, the repetition, the ritual that reinforces living in love, of continuity, and all things ethereal.

The snow stopped for a day of brilliant sunshine. The icicles melted in the frigid cold because of the loving sun. And then a flat white sky replaced the blue. Snow fell, and the atmosphere was once again pure Zen. Our tiny garden never looked more enchanted. White drifts created swirls of marshmallow fluff. Walking out the back door to catch a whiff of the crisp blanket of snow of a New England winter, I saw snowflakes bigger and more beautiful than any diamonds. Who among us knows the value of a fleeting snowflake? I came back inside where Peter and I polished brass, lit more candles, and hugged our day away. The cottage smelled of abundance. We boiled chicken stock, baked cookies, read and dined by the light of the fire and candles. We went to bed when we started to feel sleepy, awakening naturally the next morning.

The soul is not where it lives but where it loves.

— *Thomas Fuller*

Is it possible to live in love, even when there is such angst outside this peaceful village where we have found true happiness? We all need to escape into our own private haven occasionally in order to pursue personal pleasures in peace, uninterrupted, to elevate our everyday living to acts of love. You make serendipitous discoveries about yourself and your loved ones, as

Love makes you feel at home no matter where you are in the world.

well as your environment, quite by accident when you shed responsibilities, time tables, and obligations beyond your own needs and desires, even if only for a few days of escape at a time. Love is the most important inhabitant of your home. It is invisible yet always seen and felt. The love that goes into the preparation of the chicken soup becomes a sacrament when the soup is sipped together, and its goodness and nourishment have no bounds.

What we play is life.

— Louis Armstrong

The snow eventually stopped. A friend shoveled our steps and sidewalk. The sun came out, creating a magical glistening of hundreds of new icicles dangling down in front of our windows from the roof. The warmth of the sun sweetened the atmosphere, and the crisp purity of the air felt buoyant. Our love felt revived and bold. We were untired, unanxious, unrushed. Everywhere was silence except a nearby tap of a carpenter's hammer or a shovel creating a walkway for the mailman. The stillness spoke louder than words. The harmonious, melodious atmosphere, the light and brilliance burnished our souls with the same illumination. Trudging down the street to buy coffee beans and pick up the newspaper in our yellow Wellington boots, crunching high piles of cotton snow in razor cold air was exhilarating. The red bells attached to the doorknob jingled joyfully as we opened the door to our sweet cottage.

The ordinary arts we practice every day at home are of more importance to the soul than their simplicity might suggest.

— Thomas Moore

These three days we lived in another world, enlightened by our surroundings, sensing them with increased appreciation and affection. It is important to experience the epiphanies right where we are, in the flow of daily life. Nirvana and enlightenment and love aren't out there, out of reach, somewhere else. We have the potential to seek and find this spiritual bliss in the here and now by creating a loving atmosphere at home and celebrating each moment. Living in love follows the natural rhythms of our higher power when we're mindful of our feelings, making reality and our vision become one.

Living in love is a self-fulfilling prophecy, where an inspired message becomes a reality. Each individual lover of life becomes a prophet, filled with divine inspiration. Your love of self, your lover, your children, beauty, and truth come from the same force.

Each of us can create an atmosphere for loving. Our house, when loved, becomes a home, no longer inanimate, but alive. In this consciousness, life is cast in a positive light. We respect, support, honor, and trust each other. We enchant, delight, inspire, and energize each other with our zest as well as with our indomitable belief in the value of *being*.

> *Grief can take care of itself; but to get the full value of joy you must have somebody to divide it with.*
>
> —*Mark Twain*

It feels good to be kind, gracious, enthusiastic, and appreciative. All our sensibilities increase because of a greater, more enhanced perception of what we know. When we're receptive, aware of the infinite, miraculous possibilities for one human life, we open up wide to charging our lives.

The ways to achieve personal fulfillment are numerous. Acting according to our highest values, being filled with good intentions, is a real signal love is present. The passion for *being*, the rapture of always *becoming*, are powerful forces for truth and love. Make your life a flame burning brilliantly. This com-

5.

Time Alone, Together

Love takes time, privacy, silence, and sweetness.

Privacy for Two

When you love yourself and each other, when you create a home that nourishes your souls, you both naturally participate in the interplay of daily life, helping divide the labor and magnify the joy.

You have found privacy for two. You move about with ease. Nothing seems a burden because when you live in this loving consciousness, your energy is channeled on appreciation. You see with more love in your eyes as well as your heart. The sun on your flower arrangement is cause to rejoice. The painting you put in your bathroom delights you. The loving atmosphere you create uplifts your spirit, and your mood is sunny and full of cheer. Your rooms don't bore you because they're emotional balm. You love being together in a place you've created as a couple. Here, alone together, you feel a deep, sustaining, intelligence of life.

Ah! There's nothing like staying home for real comfort.

—Jane Austen

Love requires privacy. That's increasingly hard to obtain. Making real time for each other, not just squeezing in a few minutes, is critical to keeping love alive. We all live such hectic lives today that many of us rarely take time out of our busy calendars for much needed special time together. Many people have adapted so well to this busyness that they've all but forgotten the pleasures of intimacy. Going to the theater, to a movie, or to a leisurely dinner, or even just taking time at home alone together, restores us to ourselves and reconnects us to each other. When we spend time alone, our senses are reawakened. We see each other in the heightened glow of our love.

Those who live in love experience the sublime.

To live in love, we must never take each other for granted. Time alone for a couple is as important as food and oxygen. The sense of connectedness grows stronger, keeping up the vitality. You have to seize time when the children are asleep or out of the house. Those of us who have young children or grandchildren have to establish "quiet time" where you can be alone. We have a closed door grace note; everyone knocks if a door is closed. The respect for others' privacy works across gender and age. No one barges in on anyone in our home. When the girls were little we called them the "knock knocks." During nap times Peter and I on a Saturday or Sunday were free to lie on our bed and be together while the children rested. If you love someone, you show this love by wanting to be together. If you need to hire a baby-sitter so you can have a romantic date with your love, it is worthwhile. Being close, spending happy, carefree time together is priceless. This is key to staying in touch with yourself and with your love.

Recently I saw our friend's three daughters out on an adventure with a cheerful, freckled, red-haired baby-sitter. We kissed the girls in their signature red wagon and inquired about their parents: "Where are Mark and Eleanor?" "They went to Block Island for a little romance. They'll be back tomorrow night." If claiming private time with your love requires getting out of the house, do it. Go away for a night. Don't get in a rut where you feel intimacy is fading away, leaving you helpless. There will always be distractions. Just as soon as the children grow up, they have children, and the cycle continues. But in a committed love relationship, staying close physically as well as intellectually and spiritually is essential to fulfillment. There is ecstasy in keeping in mind one of my favorite poems by William Blake, "Auguries of Innocence": "To see the World in a grain of sand,/And a Heaven in a Wild Flower,/Hold infinity in the palm of your hand,/And Eternity in an hour."

The truth of any moment is always being just as we are.

— *Charlotte Joko Beck*

Peter and I are not roommates, we're lovers. We seize the time to be affectionate, intimate, and tender. This is the essence of living in love. Just as writers write, dancers dance, singers sing, and painters paint, lovers love. They seek each other's company. When two people have this close association, it is mutually beneficial. I know lovers who meet in the park or for a pizza at lunchtime just to stay connected. Lovers love to be alone together.

A minister at our local parish in New York once told Peter and me that we spend too much time together. He thought all this togetherness could lead to discord and trouble. This confused me. My mother had feared Peter wouldn't pay enough attention to me, he'd be too preoccupied with his legal practice. Neither this minister nor my mother was correct. Peter and I are instinctively drawn to each other. I think we can all be this way when we direct our attention, and never underestimate our potential to enlarge our love.

Away from the noise and bustle of a busy life, alone together we can create the tranquility that reconnects us to our most intimate, sensual selves. We can respond to each other directly; we can do what feels right to us, moment by moment. We enjoy our bike rides down quiet lanes, looking at antique houses, pointing out architectural details. We love to walk to the point, the tip of the peninsula in Stonington, sit on the rocks, hold hands while we watch the boats come and go as the sun sets. We have fun pulling weeds, watering the plants, going up to the attic to look through boxes of memorabilia, lingering at the kitchen table talking or going around the village taking pictures of gardens—these times are blissful.

You must have a room or a certain hour of the day or so where you do not know what was in the morning paper . . . a place where you can simply experience and bring forth what you are, and what you might be. . . . At first you may find nothing's happening. . . . But if you have a sacred place and use it, take advantage of it, something will happen.

—Joseph Campbell

Peter and I have reached the stage in life where we can spend an enormous amount of our daily lives alone together. It hasn't always been this way. As our life patterns changed from being busy raising children and building our careers, we've made subtle, gradual shifts in order to spend more time together. After Peter left a Wall Street law firm, he started his own firm in midtown and I joined him, paying rent for my interior design firm in the same space.

When his lease was up years later, we talked things over and chose to move both our offices to the apartment. I no longer wanted to have to work at a formal office, preferring to work from our New York home or the cottage. (Clients never come to decorators' offices, we go to their houses.) I was traveling a lot and wanted to simplify our lives. Peter's law firm did move to another building, but Peter chose to work at home also, for two reasons—home is a loving atmosphere, and we'd be together. When the children were young I'd stay home when he traveled for legal work, but once they were away at college I was able to go with him on his business trips to Hawaii, China, Hong Kong, Paris, and Taiwan. Now, we're alone at home with all the children grown and on their own, and we want to spend our nights together. If I go out of town for work and return the same evening, Peter usually doesn't join me. But if I have to spend the night away, he comes along. We haven't figured out how to touch toes and kiss each other goodnight over the telephone.

We live as lovers, and as lovers we want to be together as much as possible. We have made financial sacrifices for our love affair and have no regrets. After we were married, a wealthy Texas widow wanted me to decorate her Colonial brick mansion, but I couldn't stand to leave Peter. I had never felt this way before. I turned down the job, recommending another dec-

Theirs is the language of the heavens, the power,
The thought, the image,
and the silent joy:
Words are but the under-agents in their souls.

— *William Wordsworth*

orator. Three months later the client persisted, and Peter urged me to say yes this time. The time was right, so I did. Over twenty years this client became one of my biggest patrons, but I would never take a job that would separate Peter and me for long. We'd go together, though paying for two was considerably more expensive and clients don't pay for both of us to travel. Nor do publishers have a spouse clause covering Peter's expenses when he accompanies me on book tour! But we believe love is our compass, guiding our course, informing our destiny.

Peter and I are finally relishing this romantic, intimate, sensual time alone that most couples have when they're first married, before they have children. Peter and I didn't have this freedom until recently because when we married, we both already had young children. (We returned from our all too brief honeymoon to find a juvenile delinquent, Peter's youngest son, on drugs, and learned that he hadn't gone to school during the five days we were in Paris.) Now, we've raised and educated our children and are free to turn work down in order to live in love together. We're not running *from* each other, we're running *to* each other. Money was an important consideration with school tuitions and all the related expenses and responsibilities of having a large family, but now we've entered a new chapter where we have more freedom, being able to bring our mutual energies together.

There is no more lovely, friendly and charming relationship, communion or company than a good marriage.

—Martin Luther

Our love is the most important reality of our lives. While so many people seem restless, in a rush to fill time, Peter and I prefer to empty ourselves into each moment. We concentrate our attention on the experience, noticing the spectrum of color moving onto a white table cloth through of a piece of crystal suffused by sunlight. We appreciate this moment, ponder its depths, delight in the wonder, feeling the rapture of *being* alive.

We are happy to *be* present to appreciate the nowness, to experience, to love. If we didn't want to live this way together, we'd simply find people to see, places to go, things to do.

We lose our sense of time together, letting our conversations and our thoughts wander into new places, continuously rediscovering each other anew. To live in love together, we turn off the television, reconnecting to real life, right where we are. These gentle times are restorative to heart and soul, always inspiring us to appreciate life even more than we do. One of Peter's mottoes is "It's later than you think," written on an ancient garden wall in China. There's no time to waste when all our powers can be directed toward creating a loving life in the time that is left to us.

Hug up.

—*Peter Megargee Brown*

At a book signing in a mall in Illinois a few years ago, a woman bought one of my books and announced she would treat herself to reading it in January. "Why wait until January? That's almost two months away!" I said. "Why not this afternoon? Go home, curl up in a comfortable chair with a cup of tea, and spend twenty minutes reading." Staring at me, she confessed, "Alexandra, I'm too anxious this time of year. My mind is racing. It's hard for me to sit still. I think of all the hundreds of things I should be doing. I just can't seem to concentrate." Tears welled up in her eyes. We ended up having quite an interesting talk and when she left I felt she was going to go home, make that tea, put her feet up and open the book.

One of the reasons we work so well together is that we've learned how to handle restlessness by taking care of our personal needs. One man almost cried when he told me his wife is a jumping jack who never sits still. It drives him crazy. He can't stand the lack of contemplation and grace. The house is always a bustle, where living time is consumed with activity. His wife not only is restless, but she can't stand to see her husband sitting in a chair when there's "so much to do." He, in turn, resents being made to feel guilty about wanting to sit in a comfortable chair, unwind, and relax in his own home. Chores do eventually get done, and they should not be a constant bone of contention.

I'm a firm believer in productivity and Aristotle's doctrine of active virtue advising us to turn our inspirational thoughts into thoughtful acts. But using our physical energy to try to calm the chaos in our minds is not addressing the cause of the problem.

Cultivate more joy by arranging your life so that more joy will be likely.

— *George Witkin*

Why is it that so many people arrange their lives in such a way that they feel too nervous and tense to sit quietly in a chair and contemplate life's deeper mysteries? A house is to be lived in, not worked at. When everything is a chore—a messy room to be picked up or a sinkful of dishes to be washed—and efficiency is valued over the quality of each moment, inner joy gets snuffed out, and the beauty of daily life in the privacy of your home is fatally lost. Nervous energy is unsettling not only to you, but to others around you. Home should be our personal heaven, our all-powerful, intimate epiphany of the ordinary.

How many couples do you know who panic when they find each other alone, together with no outside distractions or appointments? This realization often happens when the children leave for college, forcing the husband and wife to face each other after years of habitual avoidance. What develops is an inability to sit still and *be* with the other person for fear of realizing that the space between you is empty, the energy dry. Are you better off living life in this frantic way, never knowing what *isn't* there? If you do, however, you also run the risk of denying yourselves the potential of what could be. Relationships, in order to remain alive and expanding, require privacy and attention. The energy between two people will remain strong only if both partners are willing to regularly spend time alone, together.

When two people can spend an entire day together doing nothing but enjoying each other, this is a positive sign. What happens when you and your love are alone for a day? How often are you? What kinds of things do you say? What do you like to do? I had a Frenchwoman as a client who once told me her husband was "fatiguing." "I can't be alone with Charles because he's exhausting. He's too intense. I need to dilute his energy with others. Oh, we're not at all alike."

When Peter and I spend time alone, together, what makes it special, so pure, is that both of us relish this time as restorative and inspiring. The positive energy between us builds as we express our whole selves in whatever we're doing and are fueled by each other's presence. One of us may be reading while the other is absorbed in repainting a window ledge, but we are united in spirit.

We become vessels of love, and in that instant of loving reciprocation we acquire the ecstasy which is timeless and eternal.

—Paul Johnson

Peter and I understand the spell would be broken if all of a sudden one of us became dissatisfied with the moment and immediately sought the undivided attention of the other. Problems usually arise among lovers when one person is experiencing a sense of insecurity that leads to a feeling of neediness, including a compulsion to control the other person's attention. The same people who hate to be by themselves cannot stand it if they are not the center of attention when another person is in their presence. They feel neglected and threatened, seemingly unaware that their behavior is exhausting. I have a friend who confided in me that every time she tries to read when her boyfriend is in the room, he interrupts her, feeling ignored. Never mind that Ted is usually deeply involved with his computer when Melissa picks up her book. Still, he insists upon her energy being focused on him and him only, otherwise he can't relax. Ironically, this desperate need for attention pushes people away, even those who love them the most.

The truth is that home is the only place of liberty.

— *G. K. Chesterton*

I know a woman who cannot sit still in a room with her love unless they are talking or being intimate. She's like an unstable molecule, moving anxiously around until it finds something else to unite with to stabilize it. But, as I said earlier, the key to intimacy is knowing how to soothe and nurture yourself, first. Without inner resources we remain in constant need of something outside ourselves to make us feel whole, and the periphery can never fill a void in our center. Once we learn how to nourish our core, the circumference expands in light and love. Love itself never saddens or is heavy, but gives you a feeling of buoyancy and joy.

I'm secure when I'm alone, and this feeling of inner completeness continues and is enhanced when I'm with Peter. When we're alone, together, neither of us senses a void that has to be filled by the other. Being together in silence is intimate. You feel each other's energy. We're fully conscious of each other's presence but in an unobtrusive, sweet way. We're not together because we don't know how to be alone, but because we're so compatible and comfortable; it's heavenly living in love. There enters a delicious mood of contentment, of incomparable well-being. We glide, enfolded in happiness. I love to be with Peter when he's absorbed in reading *The New Yorker* or the new biography of Abraham Lincoln because it allows me to be equally absorbed in William James or Carl Jung, without distractions. Everything each of us reads, writes, or imagines in these times alone, together, inspires fascinating discussions. We move about in a dream where time is suspended. Each of us creates our own perception of the ideal life we want to lead.

One sweetly solemn thought Comes to me o'er and o'er; I am nearer home today Than ever I have been before.

—Phoebe Cary

Peter and I need time to think and read. Sometimes we crave this so much we declare a "writer's workshop." In *Flights of Memory: Days Before Yesterday,* Peter wrote an essay about our times researching, reading, and writing. We give each other karma, good vibrations, feeling fulfilled by our satisfactions in the process.

We shared an enchanted day with a friend, Ray Bird, and his spouse, Anita, in Fiesole, a hill town above Florence, last July. We met because as their English teacher at Spence School in New York, Professor Bird had inspired Alexandra and Brooke to become writers. Ray and I talked for several hours about books and how we can learn about our potentialities through reading the works of highly developed minds and souls from the past and the present. We can transport ourselves anywhere in the world by holding a book in front of us, being in the company of genius and thoughtful, responsible minds. Peter and I believe books are our way to expand our love of life, empowering us to envision greater possibilities for our creative powers. We learn so much about ourselves from reading. When people ask me how I have time to read, my answer is simple: "How could I not find time to read?" I'd be half alive.

Professor Bird believes we are "becoming" through reading; the mind and the soul rise to more prominence. Over time, there is a subtle metamorphosis, a transformation of spirit. We create our own perception of life, willing it in the direction of light, beauty, truth, and love.

Peter and I spur each other on, vowing to continue to make reading a priority. As we raised the children, we read to them as all parents do, but they also observed us reading and discussing the same books. We spent evenings reading while they did their homework. I don't think it is an accident Alexandra and Brooke are both writers. They grew up in a home where they saw what happiness we derive from reading as well as writing. Peter's range of knowledge, which he attributes to literature, certainly serves him well in his legal work, but beyond that, it fills his soul with pleasure.

Silence and spaciousness go together.

—*J. Krishnamurti*

We share as a family wonderful conversations about books and life, reawakening our curiosity, increasing our hunger for life. When you try to penetrate the regular boundaries of your being through study and contemplation, to discover what is beyond your vision of life, you continuously expand your imagination. This process sharpens your pleasure and extends your healthful life.

Loving Care and Cooperation

"You take such good care of me, darling," Peter once thanked me as I was ironing his shirt. "You take such good care of *me*,"

I responded. "Aren't we lucky?" The night before Peter had heard me coughing, and got out of bed to get me a glass of water and two vitamin C tablets. "When you take care of me, I feel so loved," I whispered.

We are partners in a collaborative relationship. Living in love depends a lot on how well we remain balanced between our mutual need to be cared for and our responsibility to be caring. We all have a deep need, both children and grown-ups alike, to feel cared for because when we are, this is love in action. The heavenly surprise for me is how much Peter and I nurture each other—without the debilitating notion of keeping score.

We take care of each other in large ways and small. When one of us is feeling worried about something or going through a difficult time, we show our loving care by sitting down and listening to each other or by doing something to help; it could be making a necessary phone call or researching the solution to a problem the other is having.

Anxiety is love's greatest killer.

—*Anaïs Nin*

One of the most caring things Peter does for me is to protect my higher power by subtly reminding me whenever I get overly enthusiastic and take on too many projects; he gently suggests I slow down. We are both conscientious by nature and have commitments to others we always try to meet. But there are a great deal of demands on our time, and we help each other to set limits. Sometimes Peter will turn down a social invitation because he feels I need a moment's peace. We talk everything over. If he feels bad because of a child's behavior, I gently help him to see the bigger picture. I give support to him unconditionally. Peter trusts me, knowing I'll always be there for him.

We stick together no matter what happens, and family and friends know this.

There are hundreds of small ways we demonstrate loving care, from volunteering to do errands for each other to giving each other days off, and, as a surprise, bringing home special treats. When I took it upon myself to paint our bedroom, Peter became the master sander, ladder holder, and brass polisher. We give massages when one of us is stiff or sore, and Peter likes to rub my feet. He also enjoys picking out a few bunches of flowers at the Korean market, making little bouquets and putting them around the rooms. He always turns lights on in all the rooms and plays favorite tunes we both adore.

I am never long, even in the society of her I love, without yearning for the company of my lamp and my library.

—Lord Byron

Once when I was in North Carolina at a board meeting Peter went to Gracious Home on Third Avenue, selected a white floor lamp and walked it home as a surprise for me upon my return. I love setting up a pretty tea tray with cookies and flowers for us to enjoy. If Peter is engrossed in work, I'll empty the antique brass bucket he uses for a wastebasket, polish it, and put a white paper doily on the bottom. We select books for each other and inscribe them with love notes.

I love Peter's clothes and enjoy helping him maintain them. When I'm in the puttering mood I enjoy organizing his socks and shirts and rolling his boxer shorts. These little acts of love are seamless and effortless. Love as an energy is inexhaustible. With exercise as well as love, energy multiplies when released into action. We only increase our creative, productive powers every time we give of our true selves to another person.

When two people spend as much time together as Peter and I do, there is a rhythm and a flow to love, bringing harmony. We've learned, over all these years, how to please each other in caring ways. When we're private, we're able to increase our intimacy and affection in an environment of tranquility without irritating each other or being distracted by others. Peter is the one person I'm able to love completely. Many younger couples may not be able to spend as much time alone together, especially when they're raising young children, but it is essential they stay connected, intimate and tender so when they're able to spend time alone together, they will not meet as strangers.

When you escape from the noise of the world into the freedom of privacy, time is suspended.

Last year, Peter told me he wants to be a centenarian. Smiling, he announced, "And we'll go to Paris on my one hundredth birthday." Returning a grin, tears flowing, I responded, "I'll be there." We read in a newspaper once an expression that makes us smile: "I'm in a go mood." We are.

Peter and I have developed a loving vocabulary. We use kind, gentle, affectionate words with each other. He calls me angel, for example. We talk in a loving poetry, with love being spoken throughout the day.

Love is a gift. Often you don't have to do anything for another person but *be* loving. A smile, holding hands, a love pat, a bear hug, a tap on the shoulder, a kiss on the lips, looking into each other's eyes; *being* quiet, *being* inwardly content is *being* loving.

By quiet observation, without discussion or ponderousness, I find resolutions to many of Peter's needs as he does mine. I might draw him a bath, press his white trousers, lay out a yellow-and-white-striped bathrobe, plan a trip, buy him a colorful tie, or bring home a delightful after-shave, surprise him with tickets to a play, or lay out freshly ironed pajamas. It doesn't matter what I do, he knows I love him and enjoy doing whatever I can to please him. When you are truly loving, giving is your natural cast of mind. Giving isn't dull or weighty but fluid, refreshing, and sweet.

Without tact you can learn nothing. Tact teaches you when to be silent.

—Benjamin Disraeli

When Oprah Winfrey asked Peter if decorating is addictive, he smiled and said, "Oprah, I don't know about that, but I'm addicted to my decorator." I believe I am physiologically dependent on Peter's love. I feel grateful for the gift we're given each day to cherish: the present moment. In all my gestures, thoughts and acts, I want to lift Peter up, to increase his joy, to share meaningful times together, because I care how he feels, moment to moment.

Perhaps the greatest gift we give to each other is *time*, whatever it takes, to help one another. We contribute in whatever ways we can, never hoarding or being stingy with our resources. We love to give generously to each other; we are one, and we exchange gifts in this awareness. Erich Fromm calls this consciousness, where you are two and also one, "paradoxical logic."

The Gift of Cheerfulness

In Peter's book of essays, *One World at a Time*, he lauded what he termed my daily cheerfulness. Peter often tells me my cheerfulness colors the walls of his mind. I believe this is a great talent. Researchers are trying to figure out why some people go through life for the most part cranky, grouchy, and down, while others are cheery, upbeat, lighthearted, and exuberant. Dr. David T. Lykken, a behavioral geneticist at the University of Minnesota, wrote about happiness in *Psychological Science* magazine. According to him, "About half of your sense of well-being is determined by your 'set point' which is from the genetic lottery, and the other half from the sorrows and pleasures of the last hours, days or weeks." When you've known someone for a long time, and their disposition has *always* been one of exuberance, this is something rare. If a person's natural temperament is cheerful, others present tend to resonate in this mood, sweetening the atmosphere.

I speak the truth, not so much as I would, but as much as I dare; and I dare a little more, as I grow older.

—*Michel de Montaigne*

Cheerful people are my favorite people to be with; I never tire of their company, especially children. I love their sunny dispositions. Most people whose cheerfulness is infectious have encountered pain, sorrow, and loss. One of my best friends, who has lived through almost inhuman loss, shrugs his shoulders and explains, "What can you do?" This is the very friend who can turn my tears into laughter. Living in love requires tremendous courage and inner strength. Loss increases the value of being alive.

Erich Fromm obviously studied the teachings of the Buddha. Fromm believed, "To be fully awake is the condition for not being bored, or being boring—and indeed, not to be bored or boring is one of the main conditions for loving." Peter told me recently, "Once you enter the arena of living in love you can never retreat without suffering. The anguish you might feel if you are off your path should induce the effort to rise again to that level of elation, to a higher cadence."

If happiness is half a genetic disposition, the good news is all of us can improve the level of the other half by at least fifty percent. If we believe we can, and are willing to redirect our energies, light will flood into our hearts, and there will be a radiant glow on our path, increasing our capacity to love more abundantly.

> *The right to be alone—the most comprehensive of rights and the most valued by civilized men.*
>
> *—Justice Louis D. Brandeis*

Dr. Lykken's advice is salient and wise: "Be an experiential epicure. A steady diet of simple pleasures will keep you above your 'set-point.' Find the small things that you know give you a little high—a good meal, working in the garden, time with friends—and sprinkle your life with them. In the long run, that will leave you happier than some grand achievement that gives you a big lift for a while." Peter and I are both romantics so we're quixotic about little impractical luxuries and indulgences, knowing how good they make us feel. Be an experiential epicure!

Being There

Peter and I don't suffer from gender role-playing, so we're able to spend far more time together than many couples. Perhaps because Peter had already accomplished so much professionally by the time we married, he had more freedom to nurture and encourage me—and he did, supporting my career, sometimes at sacrifice to himself. Knowing Peter as well as I do convinces me of his lack of egotism and freedom from selfishness. His happiness is a result of a spirited, vigorous, courageous personality and character.

When I used to talk early on about my dreams, Peter would listen carefully, even though many were surprising to him and different from his own. I wanted to travel and write. Peter embraced my desires wholeheartedly, including my longing to be a writer. My lofty goals were not in any way threatening to Peter. In fact, he has been one of my strongest supporters. I had no interest in settling into a routine. I wanted to continue to explore the world, exposing the children to many cultures.

> *The skillful audacity required to share an inner life . . .*
>
> — *Gertrude Stein*

Peter f ls no self-consciousness participating in ladies' teas or weddi howers. There are at least two reasons why Peter is present rst, we are one. Second, he is equally involved with the peopl eing honored. These events are important, and by his presence, he shows love. He's never missed Alexandra's or Brooke's birthday parties since we married. Peter is always clear about what's really important. He gladly accompanies me on all kinds of tours and meetings, and I do the same for him because we've made a commitment to be together. We value each other's presence.

I can still vividly recall getting up at four o'clock on the morning was to appear on the *Today Show,* then hosted by Barbara Walters. A car from NBC picked me up to go to the studio at five A.M. Not only did Peter organize coffee and juice and accompany me to the interview, but we also picked up his son, Peter junior, along the way. Afterward, Peter invited all our children to join us in a celebration breakfast at a quiet restaurant. From that day on, I knew how supportive Peter could be. He knew what a big moment it was for me to go on national television for the first time with my first book, and by his making such a fuss over me and including his family in the event, I realized how much pride he has in me.

After a short period of deprivation, people discover suddenly that they have time again — time for being together, time for doing the things they want which somehow got crowded out.

— Eknath Easwaran

I want Peter to live an enchanted life, the life he yearns for and deserves, and he wishes the same for me. It's natural for me to turn my energies in his direction because I am sensitive to his wishes. One of my heroes, the English language genius Dr. Samuel Johnson, named the elusive source of our loving energies when he wrote, "The most useful art of all, that of pleasing, requires only the desire." Peter and I continuously discover just how much we want to please each other. We become more and more capable of perceiving and responding to external conditions as well as stimulation, paying attention and being receptive to the circumstances, attitudes, and feelings of each other. We want to be whole, solid, and strong for each other's spiritual renewal.

Our commitment to love and honor each other in our thoughts and acts opens us up to the great joy of being free to be ourselves. We define our lives on our own terms, with our personal vision of what expands us. Without realizing what was happening, when we were first engaged, our hearts opened wider to each other. Over time, we've learned how to be loving in all situations, helping each other to blossom in every aspect of our being. Just as a flower unfolds its splendor from within, or a child discovers all the possibilities for her own fulfillment, powers expand, and this process of growth and discovery, of *becoming* continues throughout all of life's chapters.

In his book *The Living Earth Manual of Feng-Shui*, Stephen Skinner describes the energies of Yin and Yang: "Yin governs the Earth, all that is negative, female, dark, water, soft, cold, deadly or still; whilst Yang governs Heaven and all that is positive, male, light, fiery, hard, warm, living and moving. Of the combination and permutation of the Yang and the Yin is formed the rest of the universe whose life and breath is ch'i."

> *Those that love most speak least.*
>
> — *George Pettie*

Both Peter and I, as do all females and males, share yin and yang energies. The more we complement each other's different energies, making up in each other what is lacking, the more instinctual approach we develop to our intimate daily lives. When we are alone, together, we unconsciously balance our energies between yin and yang, providing a vast range of new rituals and imaginative insights. There is a precious countenance, the spirit of infinite gratitude, and a refreshing sense of wonder and astonishment. We never greet a new day as monotonous.

Free to *Be*

I love the rhythms of our days. We have learned how to move in and out of each other's physical presence and grace. We can be close, cozy on the sofa together, each reading a book or newspaper or listening to music. Or, one of us may want to be alone, go to the study to write a letter, go to the Zen garden to meditate, call a child or friend, go down to the studio to paint some baskets, or go for a walk or bike ride. I may want to curl up in bed, while Peter may be off and running to meet a Federal Express deadline for a brief due in court or finish a chapter of a new book—or just pick up the newspaper. But though our immediate responsibilities and needs often pull us in different directions, our love is a constant living energy, confirming and nurturing all the beauty and good there is.

The key to finding a balance in closeness is being aware that each of you has particular desires as well as responsibilities *independent* of the other. Within the envelope of love, there is enormous freedom to come and go, because the energy of love is always connecting you. One of you could have a spontaneous enthusiastic urge resulting in serendipity. You can be reading in one room, when your mind dreams up an idea and you jump up to do something, but you don't want to disturb your love. Often, it is more thoughtful to go over to your spouse, kiss him good-bye, and tell him you're going for a walk than to invite him to come. I did this once and Peter looked up from his desk, returned my kiss, and smiled, "You're too cute. I'm coming, too." We always stay in touch, knowing where the other is, even when we're not together. If I'm at the library Peter knows I'm there. If I leave the living room to go to the village to pick up a pie for supper, I tell Peter. He does the same for me.

> *The thoughts that come often unsought, and, as it were, drop into the mind, are commonly the most valuable of any we have.*
>
> *—John Locke*

We respect each other's inner feelings, and while, occasionally, we break the silence, it is usually to offer each other a drink or some tea, or to share a kiss, a thought, or a bit of news or information. If I read or write something that makes me trem- ble with joy, I'll interrupt Peter and he'll look at me as I read him a sentence of two. There are special times when we want a hug or some out- ward expression of love. We have a special signal for these moments in our home. We say, "I need love." We drop our newspaper or book, and kiss and hug. We laugh because we both want the same thing: Love. Alexandra and Brooke say the same thing. It's a family tradition. These transitions from silence to conversing are tender. Peter's favorite word to describe our time alone is "sweet." Indeed it is.

Love makes the moment enchanted.

Protecting Each Other's Solitude

I can lose all sense of time when I'm in the flow of work or writ- ing. One weekend we had house guests from North Carolina. On Saturday morning everyone was in the dining room having breakfast but me. Peter explained that I was writing and would be joining everyone later in the morning. Then they all went off to the annual fair. You can imagine how strange it must have seemed to our friends that I was upstairs writing when they had come such a distance to see us. Later on, when Melanie and Lucie returned to the cottage with plants, herbs, some pottery, and a locally made woven basket, I invited them all upstairs to see me sitting Buddha style in bed writing. I told them I'd join them shortly.

The essence of Heaven lies not in receiving pleasure but in giving it.

—*Paul Johnson*

I've had to carve out time for my reading and writing ever since Alexandra was born in 1967. When I was the mother of toddlers I constantly woke up at five in the morning to write. At first I had to discipline myself to take this time for myself, or else I would never have it. But within three months, it became a habit and I looked forward to it, no longer needing to set an alarm clock. Unless I stay put—upstairs in the cottage or in our garden bedroom in New York—and write immediately in the morning, the muse disappears into eating blueberry muffins, watering plants, and talking out the words I should have written.

> *With thee conversing I forget all time.*
>
> —*John Milton*

This pattern of early-morning reading and writing these thirty years is my way to be alone, quiet, and collect the memories from my dreams, to muse, wonder, and imagine. In my reading and writing I'm able to be in this loving consciousness.

> *Inexhaustible wonder of the richness of this moment—Now.*
>
> —*Peter Megargee Brown*

No one would dare call me at five o'clock in the morning unless it were an emergency. Just as an artist begins by doing small, uncomplicated sketches to warm up before doing a big painting, I often begin my morning being still, thinking about my dreams; then I read to warm up before I write. Once my work is in the flow, I'm not afraid to stop. My subconscious energy is at work. I usually walk away from writing in the middle of a sentence so I never feel blocked or stuck when I come back to work.

Peter and I protect each other's solitude. If Peter is writing, I'll answer the telephone, and he does the same for me. If one of us makes a telephone call, the other leaves the room. More important, we understand how much both of us need time away from friends and family to be quiet in order to think, feel, and experience just being in a tranquil setting. Peter jokingly refers to us in our cottage as recluses. It's partly true. But this time at home is necessary to rebalance our energies. We learn much about ourselves listening to our inner voice in our solitude for

Let us animate and encourage each other.

— *George Washington*

two. A wise friend retreats from people regularly in order not to become "thin" inside. The balance between togetherness with others and separateness where we're alone together is an ebb and flow. The sun reaches the meridian and declines. The moon becomes full, then wanes. We all need to balance our time alone with our time with others to live life fully, to live in love.

Love's Blossoms

Over the years, Peter and I have enlarged our capacities to live in love. We slip in and out of each other's habits and patterns naturally. Together, our private collections of enthusiasms and passions have blossomed. We come up with playful ways of being considerate of each other's dignity, privacy, and mood. We're sensitive to each other's immediate feelings, trying to respond appropriately. Whether we go antiquing together or travel on business trips or vacations, we work things out with grace and love.

As a seed turns into a blossom with sunlight and water, through love we are transformed; beyond the here and now, time and space; we're changed by this natural process of growth and development *together.* During the interludes when Peter and I escape into each other, when we are in our own world, this transcendence intensifies. There's a syncopation, a rhythmic counterpoint to our interaction; we swoon into the moment and each other naturally, without censorship. Whether we are sharing our ideas at the table in our Zen garden or immersed in separate activities, our souls are calm and united. This is our time alone, together, and it is sacred.

6.

Keeping the Mystery Alive

Nothing in the world is single,
All things by a law divine
In one spirit meet and mingle.

— PERCY BYSSHE SHELLEY

Growing in Love

Living in love is a work of art, and someone once said that all real works of art finish in mystery.

I continue to look up to Peter with the same wide-eyed wonder as when we first met. Peter remains my boyfriend as well as my best friend and lover. And, as swans do, we have mated for life. We've put all our eggs in one basket and are watching everything hatch.

Rules of convention never applied to Peter and me, given the unusual circumstances of our union. While we were enjoying our platonic friendship as single parents, something magical happened. Because we lived near each other, the time and space opened up for us to begin to grow in love. Most couples don't begin a courtship taking children on bike rides in Central Park, but these sweet outings with Peter, Alexandra, and Brooke were the beginning of the mystery. The phenomenon that creates infinite rapture was starting to develop. There was a delightful, compassionate mood to these occasions, and over all these years they've only grown in poignancy and tenderness. What we didn't understand then but know now is how our mutual passion for

The fairest thing we can experience is the mysterious.

—Albert Einstein

children drew us together. We both have loved spending a great deal of time with our children, and they remain central to our living in love.

We rejoice whenever we can be with our children but never feel lonely or empty when they're not with us. Whether we're physically separated from them or not, we continue to feel the electricity that is at the heart of our bond. But our connection is greater than our children, more substantial than our shared experiences. Our love is more far-reaching than either of us can fully comprehend.

By pleasure and repeated happiness, So frequently repeated, and by force of obscure feelings representative of things forgotten, these same scenes so bright, So beautiful, so majestic in themselves . . .

— William Wordsworth

Love is a spellbinding mystery that is present at the beginning and grows as two souls become increasingly intertwined. There's no need to analyze why two particular people become one, and any kind of attempt at a scientific explanation or rationalization would be absurd. A loving relationship that continues to build over forty-three years, so far, is not one to be put into a box with a label. The love between Peter and me is ultimately a mystery, one we respect and don't tamper with.

With all of this love, because of the gift of grace, we continue to grow more beautiful in each other's eyes. We understand that the fountain of youth and the true source of our beauty is in the depth of our understanding and our appreciation for living vitally.

Keeping the Channels of Love Open

Not long ago, in a moment of deep contemplation, Peter told me why he had decided to marry me. "I wasn't looking for support," he said, "I was looking for you." Peter didn't need anything from me, but wanted to *be* with me. Both his former wives had broken his heart, each leaving him in ways involving betrayal and addiction. All of us who loved Peter knew how deeply he was hurting. But as he proved his capacity for suffering, he expanded his horizons for joy. If he hadn't accepted the disappointments, failures, pain, and heartbreak of his past, he wouldn't have felt free to begin a new life, to start fresh living in love.

There was nothing remote or mysterious here—only something private. The only secret was the ancient communication between two people.

—Eudora Welty

Everyone experiences painful situations that leave them brokenhearted, and most people grow beyond them with time. Whatever Peter wants me to know about his past he reveals to me in intimate moments, but I never probe. Anything I don't already know about Peter is probably too painful to recall and will remain unexplained. He's accepted his situation without a trace of bitterness. He has found happiness and contentment in *our* love, and maybe this is his reward for his years of suffering.

I have heard of too many cases where a spouse becomes hostile as a result of constant probing by his or her partner about prerelationship history. But we must remember that it is never our right to dig into someone's past to uncover the painful episodes; this is an especially insensitive invasion of privacy and never productive. We help keep the mystery alive by not mining each other's soul. When we mine, we undermine.

Whatever energy drew Peter and me together is alive and we cultivate it naturally. Marriage is a commencement, and the dynamics that evolve over time depend on two, not one. Wherever we are in our personal evolution, our growth is a process that depends on both people meeting on common ground. We live here and now, accepting each other as we are in the present, satisfied because we want what we have together. What we have is what we work with, and when we keep this energy channeled in loving ways toward each other, the love remains vital and increases.

> *Welcome, O life! I go to encounter for the millionth time the reality of experience.*
>
> *—James Joyce*

We ripen our love over a lifetime. A few years ago we spent a magical day and evening with a young couple, Mysty and Bruce, who were living in love after twelve years of marriage. Peter and I had flown to Atlanta where I gave a talk to designers, and Mysty was my host. After a fun day of work, we had a great celebration at one of their favorite Italian restaurants. There were a lot of toasts, good food, and a feeling of friendship and love. When there is no tension, how easily the channels of love connect us, two couples who were personally unknown to each other only hours before. How could we feel this close bond and affection having just met for the first time?

> *Explaining love is like explaining poetry.*
>
> *—Michael Drury*

The morning after our memorable day together, Mysty picked us up at our hotel to take us to the airport. As she drove, she laughed and said, "When we got home last night there was no heat. It was nineteen degrees outside and in our house. Rather than becoming upset, Bruce and I put on our flannel long underwear and wrapped ourselves in bathrobes, made some hot chocolate, and sat by a warm fire for an hour and a half before going to sleep.

"We weren't upset at all," Mysty continued. "We thought it was romantic. And it was. What is it that makes one couple grow more in love each day and another grow apart? Peter, tell me the secret because Bruce and I want our marriage to be as loving as yours." "Mysty," Peter began, pausing for a moment so he could answer her question thoughtfully, "we're just lucky and the rest is a mystery, don't you think?" Peter then added, in true Peter style, "Marriage reminds me of how to cook a Peking duck. First you find the duck. You and Bruce have found each other on the first round. Hold on."

Mysty said she isn't around loving couples enough. She confided in us how many of her friends are living empty marriages, where the couple seem to tear each other down more than they build each other up. I told her I believe love is a far higher calling than getting bogged down by the dry cleaning or the ring around the bathtub or the numerous daily domestic details. The thousands of hours Peter and I spend together only make me more admiring of him, more respectful and more aware of the

> *Faith is a prerequisite to enlightenment, illumination, and self-realization.*
>
> —*Peter Megargee Brown*

> *No one can explain how the notes of a Mozart melody, or the folds of a piece of Titian's drapery produce their essential effects. If you do not feel it, no one can by reasoning make you feel it.*
>
> —*John Ruskin*

175

beauty of his soul. His heart is always pointed in the right direction, even if he doesn't express his devotion by doing a series of household chores. Important things tend to get done. Peter is a happy, free spirit. He bristles at tough, aggressive women, and he purrs at sweetness. We both appreciate each other and we mutually adore doing necessary, practical things around the house, but in our own time, not under pressure. We try not to be critical of the moment to moment obligations. We are Zen, and tend to accept what is. Problems arise when one person assumes the role of emotional manager. Whenever this happens, the temptation is to feel bossy. We all want to be around a caring, tender person, not someone who administers the daily operations of the household efficiently at the expense of grace. We mutually respect each other's ability to make important decisions, even when they will lead to sacrifices or compromises, and if we seek an opinion, as we often do, we'll ask for advice, and we try to listen well.

Happiness is a mystery, like religion, and should never be rationalized.

— G. K. Chesterton

Understanding What Is Important in Our Lives

"Life is short," Peter often reminds me. I've come to appreciate this truth sooner than I might have otherwise if it weren't for his passion for being alive. As Emily Dickinson wrote, "That it will never come again/Is what makes life so sweet." Understanding and respecting the brevity of our lives is a gift transforming our whole experience of living. Flowers begin from seed, then root, stem, and blossom. We have this same regenerative power to give new life, to revitalize, to become inspired, refreshed, and renewed. Life *is* short. With that knowledge we learn not only what we do not have time for, but what we must give time to. Knowing this, you and your love may be less willing to go to as many cocktail parties or be around people who aren't passionately engaged in life.

> *My heart leaps up when I behold A rainbow in the sky.*
>
> — *William Wordsworth*

When we become clearer about what matters to us, we take a walk instead of doing the dishes. The infinite wonder of the stars and moon expand you and refresh you. And the walk helps you resolve pending questions and digest your dinner.

The passage of time together provides us the gift of perspective. When you live in love, you expand as you realize the truths, the paradoxes, and the fundamental laws of life. You appreciate how much love stretches you to a fuller, more giving capacity. The more life we've experienced together, the more appreciative we become of life's boundless blessings. We

> *Mix a little mystery with everything, and the very mystery arouses veneration.*
>
> —*Baltasar Glacian*

embrace life with full force. We enjoy the moment. We see how fragile and vulnerable we all are, yet how fierce and strong we can be for what's important.

Living changes us by making us more completely who we are. As our awareness of ourselves increases we become wiser about how to live, and our love is kept more brilliantly alive in ways we never knew were possible.

From Point to Point

All love is mysterious and, to a large degree, secret. Love allows us to learn to overcome seeing life through the narrow perspective of our own ego, and opens us up to benevolence, filling our hearts with an abundance of well-being.

We do live our lives in these seasons, these chapters, where we plan ahead, think about our own contributions, what we'll do to have fun as we're able to help others to achieve their own desires. We talk about goals at different intersections on our path. Goals change form and substance as we gain experience and grow. While Abraham Lincoln was president of the United States, he knew how long-range goals, over the period of a lifetime, can fade and disintegrate. It is comforting to remember the analogy he gave James G. Blaine, a government leader, when explaining his Reconstruction policies. "The pilots on our western rivers steer from *point* to *point* as they call it—setting the course of the boat no farther than they can see: and that is all I propose to myself. . . ." Lincoln's goals remained within his reach. He often quoted these lines from *Hamlet* when discussing matters with his law partner, William Herndon: "There's a divinity that shapes our ends,/ Rough-hew them how we will."

Let your spirit, your life, your loves burn brightly and only become more brilliant in eternity.

Our lives are steered much the way the river pilots went from point to point. Each of us is on a path directing our energies, challenging our strengths, learning what we need to learn, not necessarily what we want to know. There are no shortcuts to moving in the direction of our goals and self-expression. When we understand life as a process, going from point to point is not only far more realistic, but also enormously more romantic. We can feel good about the smallest, simplest experiences right in front of our nose. If we can stay steady on our course, moving ahead without losing sight of our vision to live in love, steering our course confidently in the spirit of our commitments, gentle sunbeams of light pour into us to guide us on our path.

We are wiser than we know.

—*Emerson*

Peter's and my commitment to love and honor each other opened each of us up to the great joy of being free to be ourselves. Without realizing what was happening, our hearts opened wide to a romantic chapter for us both. We're partners who help each other to blossom into the full colors of our personality. Until we experience this auspicious eclipse, where the sun and the moon coincide, it is hard to envision how we can resonate harmoniously into one oversoul. This coming together of feelings, emotions, desires, and dreams, is the greatest gift of life because with this, everything good potentially flows through you.

Maintaining Human Connections in Modern Times

Mother Teresa, founder of Missionaries of Charity in Calcutta, believes, "A joyful heart is the inevitable result of a heart burning with love." Pure love is altruistic. Where you have an unselfish concern for the welfare of others, you become more trusting, more loving. Are there forces in modern society that keep our love from flowing freely? In a 1995 op-ed column in *The New York Times* entitled "An Atomized America," Anthony Lewis informs us that "The average American spends 40 percent of his free time watching television—and those who watch a lot participate little." Professor Robert D. Putman of Harvard University believes television paints a negative picture of American society. He writes, "Heavy watchers of T.V. are usually skeptical about the benevolence of other people. . . . Heavy T.V. watching may well increase pessimism about human nature." Love requires relationship, commitment, and active participation in a positive approach to living well. We all watch television. We cannot blame television itself for the fact that we view it too much. Television, when viewed to excess, can result in antisocial behavior because it is a passive pastime. Love, because it is an energy, is active. In *Living Beautifully Together*, I suggested that we take the television out of the bedroom. Since then, we've experienced an explosive technological tilt. If I were to update the book, I'd add "no fax or computer in the bedroom." Lewis's essay suggests "the whole electronic revolution in communications, even while it enlarges our opportunities, has a profoundly fragmenting effect on the society. In other words, we can sit alone at our computers and interact only through electronics."

One of the deep secrets of life is that all that is really worth the doing is what we do for others.

—Lewis Carroll

In the 1980s, when I observed the disharmony of couples and families with the television blaring and children's rooms alive with rock music, closing doors was the expedient solution but harmed the fabric of family life. I was in a client's bedroom discussing end tables and lighting, and on the bed, stretched out, was the husband watching "the game" with huge earphones. His fists were cheering on his team and he was oblivious to our presence in the room until we walked in front of the big screen and he shooed us aside.

Some argue that the courtroom is not the place for television, but more important, nor is the bedroom. Technology can and should be restricted to specific places and times in order not to have it interfere with the karma of the atmosphere, not to chill the loving spirit in the air, a subtle kindness that affects us and those we love. The incessant clicking of the laptop computer on a snowy train ride one recent night interfered with the romance of the journey for the companion passengers. The noise reminded me of someone clicking their pen or smacking their gum, but the perpetrator was unaware of the annoyance.

Part of keeping the mystery alive is not to allow technology to block the channels of genuine human communication. Though technological advancements should be freeing up time for us to spend in a loving consciousness, they seem to have had the reverse effect on many of us. I find it ironic that much of technology is marketed as a means to advance "communications." Progress and efficiency is good as long as it encompasses the broad perspective. One of Daniel Goleman's observations in *Emotional Intelligence* is a warning:

> *There are three precepts by which I live: the first one is "Now": Focus on the present. The second one is "Time": Nothing really matters with time. And the third is "I do not know." Because the moment one thinks one knows, the mind becomes closed. Those three precepts are going to be on my tombstone.*
>
> *—Beatrice Wood (101-year-old ceramic artist)*

"These millennial years are ushering in an Age of Melancholy, just as the twentieth century became an Age of Anxiety." Perhaps now is an appropriate time to rethink this raging race to participate so fully in the technical opportunities available to us. If we spend more time musing over the wonders that are at hand and underfoot, maybe we'll see more sunbeams on our path to love.

None of us is going to do away with the inventions of modern life. We all enjoy our toys. But when I was a child, my parents didn't have to stay up all night Christmas Eve figuring out how to get an electronic toy to operate, because there weren't any. Telephones used to have cords so you sat or stood to conduct your conversation. Now, everyone paces up and down, and the threat of being interrupted by someone else's voice is everywhere. In the supermarket, the train, the plane, the airport, and even in restaurants and hotel lobbies, the ubiquitous cordless phone is "in our face." I'm appalled at the men walking along the street with a woman at their side who are acting vain on their cellular phones. I lose my appetite when Peter and I are eating lunch and someone at a nearby table obnoxiously makes "business" calls on a cellular phone throughout the meal. One of my favorite Italian restaurants in New York got wise and banned cigars *and* the use of cellular phones in their dining area. This objectionable behavior has become a habit with some people, and they get caught up in themselves. One of the best ways to keep the mystery alive is

> *The soul should always stand ajar, ready to welcome the ecstatic experience.*
>
> —*Emily Dickinson*

> *I wanted to gain courage by seeing the human soul's ability to triumph over everything.*
>
> —*Nikos Kazantzakis*

to become more Zen, more present, more sympathetic, more aware, skirting these so-called advances of technology. While modern equipment will continue to proliferate, we will have to become more disciplined to counterbalance it with unmechanized activities.

Being, Not Doing

Is it possible to be consumed, driven to make money, feeling vaguely guilty when we're not being "productive"? In the commercial sense, time equals money. Living in love requires us to make some major changes in the way we conduct our lives and how we think about time. In the introduction to the anthology of contemporary spiritual writing, *God in All Worlds*, editor Lucinda Vardey advises, "In this life, the search for the spiritual begins with the longing of the soul for nourishment. This longing prompts the search for meaning and goes onto the quest itself." It is our spirit, after all, that sustains us, not our bank balance, our business deals, and our investments. I enjoy money as much as most people, but I understand its place in my life. I enjoy earning money because it allows me the freedom to continue on my quest. I was amused not long ago when a wealthy, successful businessman told me: "Alexandra, you're losing me with all this quest business. You're too serious, lighten up." I adore this man, and have fun celebrating life with him, but he is living on a different conscious level because his primary passion is making

Each morning we are born again. What we do today is what matters most.

—Buddha

money, and he's very good at it. We usually enjoy what we have a talent for, and deal making is a game that puts fire in his belly. But the hot pursuit of the almighty dollar can often chill living in love.

The opening sentence of Vardey's anthology reads, "To seek is the start of any quest." I'm seeking greater capacities to reach out to others in loving ways. We're on the cusp of a new thousand-year period, and I believe we have to turn backward as we move forward, and search our souls for abiding truths about how we can and should solve seemingly intractable problems. We have a built-in drive to fill time being useful and productive. But when we overdo, overpromise, and expend our energy aggressively, we tend to become insensitive to the feelings of others. We don't take time to listen actively to what is in the heart and soul of another human being. Once we're able to elevate ourselves into the worlds of spirit that generate pure love, it is perhaps worth all the time, effort and, yes, money that is required in order to hone our love skills.

I have a funny kind of strength and confidence. Every decade of my life so far has been better than the last.

—Valentine Lawford

Machines and technology have made us greedy for more when our spirit yearns for less. We can't substitute technology for the pure energy of love. Our central nervous system can't stand the habitual pressure of unrealistic expectations and fierce competition.

The more I wonder . . . the more I love.

—Alice Walker

Have we become so material, so full of ourselves, our "things," our new, fancy gadgets, that we're unaware of the intangible forces that allow us to love what is truly good and beautiful? In *Gracious Living in a New World*, I spoke of the importance of occasionally turning off our television sets, unplugging our laptop computers, and ignoring the fax machines in order to appreciate the simple pleasures of life. Technology has extended far beyond its practical mission to the point of blocking the channels of loving energy among human beings.

> *Until we accept the fact that life itself is grounded in mystery, we shall learn nothing.*
>
> — *Henry Miller*

People should not become slaves to technology, driving themselves to work more hours. Loving energy is discharged differently, requiring our consciousness to build a higher awareness of mystery. If we automatically turn on the television or our computers before and after dinner, we may be snuffing out some of our loving potential, the softness in the air, the sweetness of the scent of lilies. Loving energy is an active force, and living in love requires attentive vitality to appreciate sensuality, nature, and romance. There is a proper time and place for everything, and living in love requires this understanding.

> *Birds don't know they're going to die. Just as well. Let them sing.*
>
> — *Peter Megargee Brown*

As a society, we seem to have lost sight of the nonmaterial wealth that is available to us in our "pursuit of happiness," that allows us to take part in the mystery. In the winter of 1995, a government shutdown due to budget gridlock resulted in the closing of the unprecedented exhibit of Dutch master Vermeer's paintings in the National Gallery of Art in Washington because it fell under the category of "nonessential" services. Lawrence Weschler, a staff writer at *The New Yorker*, argued that Vermeer *is* essential: "So essential, so close to the root of first things—decency, equanimity, free agency, fellow feeling, basic human regard . . ."

When we made our family pilgrimage to experience a show that included twenty-two of the thirty-five Vermeers in the whole world, we were moved by his exceptional, poetic sensibility. He encourages us to pause and reflect on the depth of the human experience shown in small moments of life. The girl with the pearls is waiting for a balance to come to her equilibrium. The senior curator Arthur K. Wheelock, Jr., described it in one word, "Hush." Vermeer captured human dignity in these quiet activities, reflecting deep emotions and philosophical concerns as well as a reverence for life that is profoundly felt by everyone who made the effort to go to see his pictures and who was fortunate to be there before or after the darkness caused by the federal shutdown. The experience reminded me anew that harmony and purity are possible in the conduct of one's life. We can become more calm and contemplative, and enjoy quiet reflections about human emotions. If we don't, we block the flow of loving energy from within our own hearts.

> *For human beings, the more powerful need is not for sex, but for intimacy.*
>
> —Rollo May

Who are the people who help us to better understand a way to live in love? Are they the artists, writers, and philosophers who tell us stories, paint pictures and scenes to gently lead us to a more loving consciousness? Is character such an old-fashioned word it is obsolete as an Underwood typewriter?

In order to do the right thing by others we have to be able to be in control of our own emotions. We steer our lives, hone our personal skills throughout life, and surrender beyond the sphere of our own ability to change things for the better. If we neglect to nourish our inner world with inspiration—whether it comes from time spent quietly in nature, or in reading wisdom of the ages, or by studying and appreciating art, or listening to fine music—we will atrophy spiritually. Life is a process toward pure love, pure spirit, where we accept life's graces, and try to do whatever is decent under the particular circumstances right before our eyes. We can't neglect to nourish our own spirit in the hectic rush of a clamorous contemporary life.

Timeless Symbols of Love

When I was sixteen and started studying interior design I had an architect professor who taught us to strive for everything organic. He wanted us to use materials of the earth, rather than synthetics. If we were to use a plastic laminate he urged us not to try to fake wood or marble, but use a solid color. This advice about using organic substances is wise. Following his advice, I try to seek in life what's real. Part of the mystery is the subtle, loving tenderness that goes into everything we do to elevate the action from a chore to a grace note. The more organic our food, the healthier we become. We are nourished spiritually as well as physiologically when we celebrate a banquet with loved ones. The food and drink is part of a greater whole—the atmosphere, the table, the colors and textures, the flowers, fruit, candles, and music coalesce into an ambiance of divine proportions. Peeling a juicy pear, breaking off a crust of bread, having a piece of ripe Brie and toasting with a white

Burgundy in the sweet pink glow of the fire can do more to keep the mystery alive than a new car.

The Accumulation of Loving Energy

Sometimes people inquire if we have a dog or cat. Unfortunately, we don't now. Our travel commitments would force us to abandon them often, and we love animals too much to do this. Peter knows how much I adore animals, particularly dogs. At lunch on one of our snow days he inquired about my favorite pet, a sweet, happy puppy named Chumily. When we moved from Weston, Massachusetts, to Westport, Connecticut, I was five and Chumily was a few weeks old. Few things are more wonderful for a child and adult than to be able to love an animal who loves you back. A rush of emotion came to me as I remembered my cocker spaniel puppy being run over by a car on Ludlow Road, in front of my eyes. "Here Chumily, here Chumily," I cried. The next thing I remember he was dead. It was awful. I was nine and he had been hit by a car while he was running to me. Peter gently asked, "When did you ever get over the death of Chumily?" Pausing for a moment, I then told Peter how I felt forty-five years later. "Chumily was a blessing and I hope and pray I will never 'get over' him. He lives on in my heart, my mind, and memory. I think about him often. He is a part of me and always will be." Every dog we've lived with, every cat, every parrot, each plant we've nourished, every gar-

Only through love do you receive the gift of grace.

den we've tended, adds to the spirit of our present day life. All the people we love, whether they have died or are still living, are always connected to us through loving energy. I'm grateful for all the love others have brought and continue to bring to our consciousness. Love transcends death, and is everlasting. This is part of the mystery.

Knowing Our Higher Selves

Are we going to get off our path from time to time? Are we going to hurt, seeing everything from the narrowness of our own self-pity? When someone's behavior is "unacceptable," can we be tough and still be loving? Are we going to scowl rather than smile? Are we going to feel jealous and guilty? Will there be times when we are full of impulsiveness and rationalizations? Will there be times when we feel overburdened and put upon? Will we become upset? Will there be times of turmoil? Is it possible to avoid anger? Or, if we can't, will we be able to play fairly, and

I love the unpredictability of life. It keeps you nimble.

—*Peter Megargee Brown*

have it be "appropriate," as Aristotle advised us? Are there any concrete benefits from arguments and confrontations? What are some of the ways we can expand our vision? How can we intertwine more positive energy into people who tend to have a difficult temperament? Can we remain loving when someone close to us is not? Can we change our way of thinking, rechanneling our energy over time? Can we learn to listen to the other person's point of view and hear fluid realities? How can we be a more supporting partner to our spouse, a more effective coach to our children? How can we be a more loving boss? How can we pursue our own needs, spending enough time reading, stretching our minds, bringing in new diamonds, emeralds, rubies, and sapphires into our thoughts so we become more inspired, more creative, more loving?

It would be impossible to love anyone or anything one knew completely. Love is directed toward what lies hidden.

—Paul Valéry

What is love? I muse. The mystery is in the questioning. Love is acceptance, friendliness, and devotion, and so much more. Love means we have an affinity for someone. When we have loving energy we want to have felicitous, not infelicitous language toward others. Love comes from *within* you, not from *without,* and only if your own heart is at peace and in a state to receive grace.

How can each of us learn to increase our capacity to love? Our psychic and emotional stability relies on our striving to be wholly ourselves. Lucinda Vardey discusses the process: "This is the treasure found at the end of any spiritual quest: that with the right ingredients of wisdom discovered on the way, we can joyfully live in the perfection of being wholly ourselves." What we learn gradually is that what we are thirsty for, we already have, and all we need to do is get in touch with our unique human heart and let its radiance illuminate all we think, feel, and do.

Whatever appeals to the imagination . . . wonderfully encourages and liberates us.

—Emerson

Love Is *Here*

I used to have to go to a church to light a candle, but now every-place can be a place of ritual and sacrament. I used to need to be in a garden to smell the roses, but now I can be calm wher-ever I am, because I understand that living in love is a state of mind that requires a healthy, optimistic outlook with a rich abundance of energy from light.

To keep the mystery alive, we must appreciate our exis-tence. We're here for a heartbeat in the span of time. By paying attention to the lessons we can learn right on the playing fields and in the schoolrooms of our everyday lives, we'll gradually understand more of the subtle nuances of a spiritually gener-ated life. I've spent countless hours in quiet repose, question-ing, contemplating, and experiencing little revelations. I've paid attention to the gentle nudging of my spirit, the grandeur of a flower, the majestic beauty of the sunset, and the ability of one curious soul on a quest to make its natural connection to the boundless universe.

An Eternal Flame

Last year I was at a celebration, sitting at a table with four crystal candlesticks that held heavenly seafoam green candles. The husband, our host, noticed they weren't lit and went to get a match. He was immediately scolded by his wife who said, "We don't light candles until after dark. It is considered vulgar." These generational myths are lessons in patience. I was itching to light those four candles and feel the inner glow.

I thought, *Lighten up, brighten up, and light the lights. Let's celebrate.*

My mother loved to light fires and candles, and I grew up feeling an irrepressible urge to light candles everywhere, not just in large, dark, European cathedrals, though Peter and I love to do that, too. Expressions of warmth will bring us visceral pleasure and touch us with mysterious feelings of collective ritualized greatness. Lighting a candle can be a larger-than-life expression of transcendent emotions, symbolic of our innate urge toward clarity, purity, and love.

> *Every moment you remain alive is a miracle.*
>
> —*Eknath Easwaran*

Thank heaven most of us are beyond rigid social rules that limit our enjoyment of an easygoing atmosphere in the privacy of our own home. Life is so fragmented and there are so many facades and out-of-date myths that could debilitate our innate urge to live with effervescence. When I began decorating I was told by people of authority that no one of taste ever used anything but off-white candles. I grappled with this dull rule. Only at holiday times were red or green candles acceptable, and more recently gold and silver. Gradually, however, stores began to stock colored candles, and now we can enjoy a wide range of breathtakingly beautiful colors. We select from beeswax to candles handmade in Sweden. I feel the same way about candles as I do stationery. You splurge on something

> *Through love, through hope, and faith's transcendent dower, We feel that we are greater than we know.*
>
> —*William Wordsworth*

lovely and enjoy sharing it with others. A lit candle brings joy to everyone. We have some fat sturdy candles Alexandra buys at a shop in Georgetown, and I buy a few pairs at a time at the Pottery Barn, Felissimo, and Henri Bendel in New York City. Even hardware stores stock a variety of colored candles.

I continue to be infatuated by fire because it is energy and light. We sometimes light colorful candles at the breakfast table. When we're in the kitchen, we light a chubby one on the old farm table. There's a light in the ceiling above but the candle brings emotional comfort and a feeling of immediacy. What is so mysteriously spiritual about a pretty, graceful candle with flickering light illuminating us and bringing us serenity? The thousands of candles I've lit over all these years bring me hope and faith, and always transformation. They activate the circuitry of the mystery, fusing the contradictions, making polar opposites complementary. Symbolically, lit candles awaken your loving, light-filled energy, offering sublime promise of exultant moments. We tend to look into and through a candle.

Love raises common thoughts to exalted, mystical transformation.

Candles calm us down and arrest our attention. We are alone in our thoughts when we gaze at a candle, even when others are near; we are lost in our own dreams and visions; our imagination takes great leaps of elation. While we are wrapped in an uplifted countenance, out of time, out of body, we experience a mysterious metamorphosis from a lower consciousness to our higher self that generates more light from within our human psyche, reverberating loving energy. Enveloped in incomprehensibility, we acquire a fresh inner awareness of universal love.

As hot colored wax drips down the side of the candle, I play with it, unannoyed it has melted onto the brass candlestick, and then the fruitwood table. Concentration on the immediacy of the moment makes me smile as I feel enclosed in a circle of love. I have a sense of the sustainability of love. Some people claim they get their best ideas while in the shower. Perhaps mine and yours come in the pink glow of a candle. Here, silence becomes reverence—for life, for truth, for light, for increasing loving energy in all directions. To keep the mystery alive we should have lots of private rituals, little playful moments where we create mini-celebrations and ceremonies that accumulatively add up to powerful life forces moving our energy upward, into the light.

In the river of life, two currents flow in opposite directions. One, on the surface, flows toward sorrow, toward sickness, toward bondage. The other, beneath it, flows toward happiness, health and freedom.

—Ancient yoga text

Think of the straightness of a candle. If it is crooked it is dangerous, and could set our house on fire. Or it may fall, and the flame will go out. But, when straight, the plume of fire is at the top, with heavenly light. Think of yourself as that straight pure light. It was my artist friend Joan Brady who told me, "Think of a lit candle in the center of your soul." This image is a metaphor for living in love.

We will all fall short of living in loving energy. There will be dark times when we're stuck on our path, and we feel muddled as we struggle for unity, as we try to find our way. But, what's important is to seize every fresh opportunity to redirect our energy, and do this together. If we feel our lives are a drop of water in the ocean, let our drop be as refreshing and clean as humanly possible. While we can't cure the problems of the world, we can heal our own soul. I believe in the power of each individual to grow in faith and understanding; to know that the soul, while we're alive, is housed inside our physical body, and though invisible, is just as in need of attention as our flesh and bones and our automobile or air conditioner.

Happiness is not a horse, you cannot harness it.

—Russian proverb

When we're ready to light our own flame, one candle in the darkness can lead the way toward light, just as a single star can pierce a black sky. We keep the mystery of loving energy alive by lighting candles in the wilderness, being silent, being present, listening well, being patient, accepting, and loving. By directing our energies to our own higher power, we're able to lighten the burdens of others, rather than add to them. While we're far from being saints and there aren't many Mother Teresas among us, at least we can improve the karma surrounding us. We can charge the wavelengths in the atmosphere with positive energy. As our own ch'i increases, we'll not only be more loving to ourselves, our spouse, children, family, community, and in our work relationships, but also in our dealings with people of different faiths and beliefs. If

Mystery is at the core of love. That's why there is so much speculation about its energizing force. Let us then be inspired to transcend to the highest level of love through the mystery itself.

—Peter Megargee Brown

you believe there's too little love around, the mystery is alive inside each of us, the love is there, ready to come out.

The mystery has been the same through the ages. Each of us will be given a series of challenges throughout our lives. We have to be aware of the direction of our energy, whether our candle is lit, providing light, or snuffed out, keeping us in the dark. Silently, wish something wonderful for someone else.

Love is a divine revelation, secret, personal, mysterious, and boundless.

Everyone has a story—think of it as a love story. Miraculously, mysteriously, you become the recipient of this loving gesture. The giving *is* the receiving, the love you bring out from your own heart radiates this joy and grace inside you.

This giving of love is what essentially keeps the mystery alive. When we give naturally, genuinely, from our own spirit, not seeking anything in return, but thinking loving thoughts, followed by loving acts, we are in the flow of divine love, and we are lifted up, expanded, elevated, and exalted. Anyone who feels love is too difficult to maintain is mistaken. Love is not a machine that can break down or an object that becomes obsolete. When I grow old, will you stop loving me? We can't be fooled into thinking two people who love each other in their youth will inevitably grow apart in their old age. We don't stop loving our children when they grow up, why should we stop loving each other? I've know Peter all my adult life. But I didn't know that during the quiet, gentle course of our friendship we were planting the seeds for lifelong love.

The ancient Egyptians crowded their tombs with exact replicas of all the good things of this life to persuade themselves that continuity of living and enjoyment was a fact.

—*Paul Johnson*

Because Peter and I are students of Zen, we don't try to dissect the mystery, analyze or criticize it; we thrive in it.

We have a consciousness that has the energy to rise above

mediocrity and negativity inside us. The mystery is kept alive by continuously opening up to this rejuvenescent source and power, where we're able to replenish our spirit whenever we wish, wherever we are. Everything you need to give and receive love already exists within you. Living in love is the essence of life. Your power to love all the goodness of life will open to you. Love is our gift. Living in love is the way.

7.

The
Eternal
Honeymoon

Love is a symbol of eternity.
It wipes out all sense of time,
destroying all memory of a
beginning and all fear of
an end.

— ANNE-LOUISE DE STAËL

Unexpected Honeymoon

Several summers ago, the children asked if they could use our Connecticut cottage for a "friends weekend" during the August village fair in Stonington. Without a moment's hesitation Peter responded, "Definitely, and I will take your mother on a romantic weekend escape." I thought Peter was thinking about a weekend of matinees and lovely dinners in New York, the kind of weekend when we enjoy dressing up and doing the town. That's always a treat but it wasn't exactly what I had in mind during this extremely hot summer. But it wasn't to New York where Peter's imagination leapt. "I think your mother and I will go to Bermuda," Peter added. A thrill went through my body.

I felt the joy of the girls coming here to this sweet village, enjoying the cottage with friends, Brooke participating in the local fair. I thought about continuity, about how certain places awaken our romantic powers, about Bermuda being a choice place for love.

What is important is that one is capable of love. It is perhaps the only glimpse we are permitted of eternity.

—*Helen Hayes*

Everything in nature, each place we travel, and all the people we meet provide fertile opportunity to find thousands of ways to show love, to find pleasure, to appreciate, to wonder, to feel blessed and enjoy ourselves and our world. When we're able to take whatever time necessary to know our true nature, through quiet contemplation, concentration, and a raised consciousness, rising above all that is negative, we redirect our energy into living in love. When you reach the soaring level, you feel astonishing grace.

*How do I love thee?
Let me count the ways.
I love thee to the depth
and breadth and
height
My soul can reach.*

—*Elizabeth Barrett Browning*

Souls living in love, with few exceptions, are passionate, directing their energies toward revering, preserving, and creating beauty. They have a point of view, a personal style about almost everything. (This living energy requires a certain commitment to do the best we can while we are healthy and able, to nourish and respect our talents and use them productively in order to increase our sense of pleasure in the process of everyday living.) They embrace the miracle of life with profound awe and respect, widening their range of appreciation, recognizing the quality and magnitude of their potentialities and life's vast possibilities. They realize, and are thankful for, their awareness of the gift of life, and their energies go toward increasing the value of each moment.

Here Peter and I were, after more than twenty years of growing closer, off once again to the place where it all began: blue sky, pink coral sand, turquoise and seafoam green, pink bougainvillea—beautiful Bermuda. When Peter and I first married, in 1974, we spent the second part of our honeymoon on this enchanted island where time is suspended, where you live in love, in light and beauty. And though we've returned to

Bermuda regularly for holidays with the younger children, this trip felt different. Now we would return alone as a couple with a lifetime of love between us. We felt a sense of renewal, anticipating *being* together. This time it felt as though we were on another honeymoon.

This reinforced my belief in the eternal honeymoon. As others believe in being born again I believe in living in love. William James, in his virtuoso spiritual analysis, *The Varieties of Religious Experience*, wrote that some people are born only once, while others need to be born twice to become themselves. I believe in the power of love's need for renewal, for inspiration, and change of scenery. I think second, third, fourth, and fifth honeymoons are a sound idea. I also believe when you live in love the flame grows more and more brilliant. For me, this particular honeymoon was a regenerative experience where the world was elsewhere and we were held in an ecstasy of intense joy, rapture, and astonishment. Our days and nights were enchanted, our compatibility binding us in eternal love.

> *We speak of what is; not of what might be.*
> —*Robert Browning*

Bermuda's expansive beauty always makes me feel free: free to walk barefoot on the beach; free to dance under the stars; and free to wear the thinnest transparent clothing over my bathing suits. Bermuda never fails to make me feel utterly, sensually alive.

> *For love is heaven, and heaven is love.*
> —*Sir Walter Scott*

Once Peter made his announcement I went into a reverie every day of the seven weeks before we left, dreaming about the sweet cottage we would rent on the south shore of this paradise island. Peter warned me not to lose my head, but I couldn't help it—and I loved every blessed minute of anticipation. He'd wink at me and say, "It could rain," or, "There could be ants in our bed." But nothing could stop my imagination from humming.

I love Peter more each day because of this collective sense of accumulative wisdom and love. "Why do I love you more now than then? Perhaps because the human process of learning is cumulative, just as the formation of the coral reef." Peter believes mutual love is gloriously unique and treasured for all its limitless expressions. Peter and I think seeing beauty through each other's eyes can double our enjoyment, show us more beauty than the first time we observed it ourselves. This is the maturity and mutuality of love. We're more patient and therefore more perceptive, more appreciative.

> *Those who love deeply never grow old; they may die of old age, but they die young.*
>
> —*Sir Arthur Wing Pinero*

Our granddaughter Julia is mature far beyond her chronological age of ten. When I'm with her I feel I'm in the presence of an illuminated soul already living in love. Her music isn't rock 'n' roll but a master symphony. When she paints, her colors are a Matisse palette; when she talks, you listen and really hear. Her ability to live in love is profound. When I ask her a question, her answers are deep. Sometimes I'm hearing words uttered by a saint. I think of my grandfather, my aunt, and John Coburn, and believe she is a spiritually enlightened soul. Her sense of engagement in life on this high beam is rare in someone who has lived for only a decade. She is true to herself, and her powers are great.

> *Happiness is not a state to arrive at, but a manner of traveling.*
>
> —*Samuel Johnson*

Some catch on at ten or younger, others learn more slowly. In the uncertainty of our time on earth, knowing life is all too short, it is wise to begin now to redirect your energies toward gaining a more loving, giving consciousness. An attitude centered in light and affirmation is positive, vibrant and inspired. We all cast a spell over others. Let ours be one of enchantment, charm and delight.

Life, liberty, and the pursuit of happiness . . .

— *Thomas Jefferson*

We are in a time in history where we will have to regularly replenish ourselves spiritually so we become more whole in a broken world. We're here to add light, not point at the darkness. Love *is* light.

Ever since I grew vegetables, fruits, and flowers I've never been able willingly to settle for anything but the freshest, most alive, because of their "life force." We are, to a great extent, what we eat as well as what we read, see, and experience. When our body is in optimum health, we experience well-being, we're free to deepen and understand more of our spiritual nature. If we seek out the best, the freshest food for our bodies and the beauty of flowers to feed our soul, if we read the finest books by the greatest minds, in order to nourish our famished souls, if we spend a large portion of our time *being*, not doing, suspended in this higher awareness, our living in love will increase exponentially with every breath of air we inhale.

There is surely a piece of divinity in us.

— *Thomas Browne*

Some people yearn to find this profound place in their soul, and are willing to redirect their entire lives in order to be born to this loving energy. Julia is someone who only needs to be born once. Yet many people need to be reborn into the divine force of love.

When Julia and I discussed what I would say at a spiritual conference in Denver, Colorado, her answer was simple. "Alexandra, tell them to always be themselves and be loving."

Life has to have a sense of fun, a lilt, a swinging of spirit.

—*Patricia Corbin*

My flight was canceled due to a storm, and I arrived having had only two hours of sleep. The suitcases came just as I was leaving the hotel room to give my talk, so I jumped into some clean, though wrinkled, clothes and was off. In a room full of five hundred people from fifty states I began with the statement, "There are two choices in life. We can dwell on the dark side and all that is negative, or we can choose the light where there is positive energy and love." At the end I concluded, "We really only have one choice, and that is to make the commitment to the light so we can live in love."

The leading English historian and journalist Paul Johnson has analyzed the quality of love. He writes with precision, "One of the principal objects of the universe was the exploration of love, to its ultimate possibilities. . . . Without love, the universe makes no sense at all. Love is its creative principle, its sustaining principle and its energizing principle."

When the mind is present in the heart, we call it happiness.

—*Betty Sue Flowers*

I had planned for the weekend in Bermuda with the care and intensity of a bride. I thought of all the gossamer dresses, my favorite feminine cotton robes and wraps that I would bring. I even planned what I'd wear to dance on the terrace after dinner. I had everything laid out, ironed, and folded weeks beforehand. Even the silk bandannas for the straw beach hat were color coordinated! I knew Peter would pack at the last moment, throwing whatever was handy into his suitcase. Peter likes all his clothes, and sometimes forgets that dark-colored socks are more appropriate with a dark suit. I enjoy seeing Peter in lively colors when he's not wearing a suit and being a lawyer. Having carefully planned my clothes, I asked him to select his favorite bathing suits, polo shirts, and ties. The planning extended to what I'd bring to read.

Love is the only gold.

—*Alfred, Lord Tennyson*

My clothes were a feast of color. As the French fashion designer Yves Saint Laurent said, "How do I choose colors? I just put on a Mozart symphony and I dream." I dreamed of this romantic island escape as a celebration of love, light, and beauty; I had a desire to be seductive as well. I felt emboldened. More mature and confident, I was experiencing enthusiastic vigor and liveliness. I hurled myself into this adventure with élan. I had one of my favorite dresses altered in just the way I'd always wanted to. This deceptively sensuous black cotton dress has a sassy balloon flounce over a slightly longer straight, tightly fitted skirt. I decided to eliminate the bottom material entirely so the skirt would end at the balloon pouf. How can a fifteen-year-old cotton dress be so fresh and new, so happy? I packed some colorful Thai silk sashes to tie

There is no end to the hope that is in us.

—*John Bowen Coburn*

at the waist. My clothes became moving art in edible shades. I felt the tingle of iridescent shades of cyclamen, mint green, aqua, emerald, aquamarine, pimiento, and lavender blue. What arabesques of textiles, colors in subtle designs and details, increasing my expectations! I envisioned each day, every scene as though I were a film producer directing a love story. I couldn't believe how much fun I was having.

I decided I was indeed a princess, Peter was my prince charming, and we were living a fairy tale. Bermuda would be living inside a Roger Mühl seascape, landscape, and still life. I felt liberated. We'd raised the children. They were now on their own. We felt the blessedness of continuity, where each new generation makes their own fresh contributions, putting their own spin on the magic, mystery, and miracle of being alive. This feeling of jaunty self-confidence, of buoyancy and cheerfulness, made me smile, gleam, quiver with de-light.

In no love story I have ever read is the character ever tired.

— Roland Barthes

I kept our plans to myself the way a bride and groom keep certain details of their honeymoon to themselves. Privacy is so much a part of romance. I'd catch myself in a whirl of elation, feeling a heightened sense of my femininity, sensuality, and abandon. These feelings rise up in us because we want them to, we conjure them up in ourselves through our excitement, our past passionate experiences, and our understanding of what it takes to awaken our sensual spirits.

Our cottage never felt so sweet the day before we left on our romantic island escape. Peter and I spent several hours puttering around the rooms so they would look nice for Alexandra and Brooke for their "friends weekend." I enjoyed making little flower bouquets for the bedrooms. I love putting fresh sheets on a bed, and in summer I use pastel seersucker coverlets, folding an antique quilt at the foot, making the room look intimate and inviting.

I'd mowed the grass in the early afternoon, one of my favorite tasks. It takes only a few minutes and makes me feel rugged. The smell of fresh-cut grass wafted in the sea air is heavenly. We were packed and ready to go, but were feeling so cozy, that even the joy of this Bermuda holiday was bittersweet. When we go away, we renew our love of home. (My friend Estelle made the mistake of planning a trip to Europe when her rose garden was in full bloom. She returned from the airport at once and never left on her trip.)

We both had grilled swordfish from nearby Block Island for dinner, something we can't get in Bermuda. I have a love of place syndrome where I literally want to scoop up the entire cottage in my arms and bring it with us wherever we go, even Bermuda. But I transport the feeling through the colors of our clothes we pack. I bring a tote bag brimming with touches of our cottage. I include our blue stationery with the white scallop shell, several colorful pens from my Zen room, a handful of favorite art postcards, a flowered elbow pillow, and a half dozen snapshots of the children and scenes of the cottage. The straw hat I wear around the village I'll bring to the beach.

> *It is, after all, not how long we live but rather the quality of our lives that gives us energy and joy.*
>
> —*Peter Megargee Brown*

We set two alarm clocks, just to assure us we wouldn't oversleep and miss our early morning flight. But when we're leaving for what we know will be such a fun trip, we sleep lightly out of pure delight. When the moonlight shines in our bedroom, I feel touched by romance. How could we be so fortunate as to dance under the stars and moon of Bermuda twenty-four hours from now? I smiled to myself, and remembered Peter's warning, "It could rain." Hugging in our bed, with four windows bringing in the twinkling sky and moonbeams illuminating the room, life temporarily was a dream.

"Sweet dreams, darling." "Sleep well, my love." My thoughts swung from our cottage in bucolic Connecticut, where honeysuckle and roses cling to fences and our village has its annual fair, to the blue morning glories, fuchsia bougainvillea, and yellow hibiscus blazing the island with color, contrasting against the turquoise-aqua foam of the sea, the coral sand, and the calm sea breeze, the sparkle and energy of the sun on the water, in the tranquility of an island paradise. I fell asleep in this flirtatious soft mood of peacefulness and contentment.

> *I dream my painting,*
> *and then I paint my*
> *dream.*
>
> — *Vincent van Gogh*

The morning arrived, and Peter asked, "Sweetheart, how would you like it if I swept you away to Bermuda this morning?" "I'm packed and ready to go. Hey hey," I answer, snapping my fingers.

Informed by Dreams

I had begun to dream a lot of vivid, detailed scenarios, picturing the scenery, in those weeks before our flight, placing me deeper, more viscerally in another realm of experience. I love dreams. They bring a special poetic power to our lives. I don't think dreams are simply random firings of the brain, but a surfacing of truth, a part of ourselves we would otherwise not know because it is usually disrupted or diverted by rational thought. A strong dream is as moving an experience as many waking moments of life. Life itself, so fleeting, so mysterious, and so beautiful, sometimes seems, in full context, a glorious dream.

My dreams aren't separate from my awake reality. The only difference is that I'm not in control of my subconscious. I don't call it forth, or manage it, but I am fascinated by the powerful visions I experience when I'm asleep. Often my dreams inform my writing. I awaken fresh from sleep and, inspired by my dreams, greet each new day listening to the twittering of the birds outside the window and the song in my heart before I put pen to paper.

Peter and I changed the pink-and-white-ribbon-patterned sheets on our bed, replacing them with a bold blue and white stripe for guests. We selected a white coverlet and a favorite blue and white quilt for the foot of the bed. We had laid out our clothes the night before—white slacks and blue blazers. I laughed when I saw the matching outfits. "Are we losing our core identity, dressing alike?" We put a flag up to welcome the guests, some due to arrive that afternoon. And we were off.

> *I cannot pretend to feel impartial about colors. I rejoice with the brilliant ones and am genuinely sorry for the poor browns.*
>
> — *Winston Churchill*

In just a few hours, we'd be having a swim, followed by a delicious lunch on a terrace overlooking the sea. I imagined this one blessed day would end by our dancing under the moonlight and stars, touching, kissing, hugging, and loving each other as if for the first time. I did a little reading on the plane, but it was hard to concentrate because my mind and heart had made the transition from our cottage to our Bermuda home. How I appreciate anticipation, creating mental images, wondering, fantasizing, daydreaming. For five days we'd live in love with no outside obligations. The girls knew where to reach us if there was an emergency but no one else was told about our secret escape. I felt naughty, I was so happy. Did I fool myself into thinking I was having a mysterious affair? What was the mystique? How could I feel this splendid? Is happiness a mirage? Can two gray-haired people who have been together for all these years fly off to an island, feeling effervescent, romantic, passionate, and loving? What sustains our enthusiasm? What is happening to us? I felt a sense of oblivion, a feeling that resonates in good times shared. Does Peter experience the same indulgent, extravagant behavior? Why do I find his temperament so appealing?

> *My bags are packed.*
>
> *—Pope John XXIII*

Whenever we're on an airplane we hold hands for takeoff and landing, a ritual that began as we flew off to Paris together the evening we were married. Because of my tennis elbow, we each have aisle seats. The stewardesses see the connection and sometimes remark, "Are you on your honeymoon?" Peter always nods, "Yes, we are."

As we approached Bermuda the view was all radiant light, celestial blue sky and turquoise-aqua sea. We held hands a bit earlier than usual, looking out the window together, both sensing that we *were* on our honeymoon. The stewardess knew it, and everybody seemed to smile knowingly at us.

I live my life with the understanding that the more love we give away, the more abundantly we receive love. There's an unconscious reciprocal altruism that naturally enters into our hearts. I love feeling happy. Who doesn't? The thoughts of love we have toward others reflect back to us, as a lingering illumination. What you give away, you receive. What you let go of, you are able to have and hold. The man sitting next to me was noble and beautiful. The more I'm with Peter, the more goodness I feel. Peter is more handsome and sensuous now than when we found our love a quarter of a century ago. Or was it twenty years before that when we met at the tennis court? Marriage doesn't start as a tabula rasa. I believe I've grown more in love with Peter gradually, ever since we met.

I unbuckled my seat belt, looked out of the plane onto the azure, ultramarine, indigo water, and felt that familiar thumping of my heart's delight. I felt as though we had been magically plunked down into this paradise. My eyes have never become jaded by the dazzling intensity of the energy that color pumps into my soul and spirit. Seeing the sparkling light on the water made me think of Emerson's words: "The great principle of Undulation in nature, that shows itself in the inspiring and expiring of the breath; in desire and satiety, in the ebb and flow of the sea; in day and night; in heat and cold; and, as yet more deeply ingrained in every atom and every fluid, is known to us under the name of Polarity—these 'fits of easy transmission and reflection,' as Newton called them, are the law of nature because they are the law of spirit."

> *The quick, spontaneous laugh of a person who has secrets that are still worth keeping . . .*
>
> —*Brendan Gill*

Peter and I held hands as we waited on the customs line. Taking our passports, the customs woman smiled, "Is this your first visit to Bermuda?" "No," Peter smiled in reply, "we came here on our honeymoon." Then, while everyone in line behind us could hear, he told her he came to Bermuda in 1937 with his family. As she examined all the Bermuda stamps in our passports, she smiled again. "I can see you're still on your honeymoon. Have a great vacation."

When we reached our cottage on the beach we opened the door wide, inhaling deeply as we absorbed the reality of being enveloped in this splendor. We know this place well and we know why we love it so—just as two people come to know the things about each other they most love. For me, it's Peter's radiant smile, his infectious enthusiasm, his sense of play, and love of beauty and color.

Living in love is the highest octave of the miracle of our life.

—*Peter Megargee Brown*

When it comes to having fun, Peter and I are often of one mind. We both reached into our suitcases for our bathing suits for our first plunge. We were both starved, but first we craved a splash in the sea to turn our bodies onto the hypnotic rhythms of the surf, to tussle with some waves, play in the foam, and let the waves toss us to the pink sand. (In Bermuda every sense is heightened and everything I see is an element in a poetic wheel of color.)

I shed my blue blazer and white slacks. I slipped into a periwinkle tank suit, then put on a seafoam-green cotton sarong. While waiting for Peter to put on his bathing suit, I unpacked my tote bag, placing several of my colorful file folders in a fan on the round table. I'd brought some pink-and-white-striped envelopes given to me by Peter's daughter Andrée as a gift. I put the pad of paper next to the telephone, a rainbow of the same colors as the Bermuda sky and water. I unpacked a few things and came across a two-inch square of mint green glycerin soap Brooke had given us as a going-away present. I took the clear plastic off the bar of soap and pressed it to my nose, smelling the deliciously refreshing fragrance called "Heaven." (The open windows of the Stonington cottage bring in the fragile sweet smell of jasmine mingled with the scent of ocean spray.) I unpacked a few colored glass marbles with flat bottoms purchased at a Park Avenue craft fair at the Sixty-eighth Street armory. I enjoy playing with them when I write. The primitive nesting instinct surprises me delightfully. I looked through the dozen art postcards I brought on this trip, including Matisse, Monet, Cassat, and van Gogh. They're fanned out on a dish to be relished as a traveling art mini-collection that doesn't need to be insured.

Energy is Eternal Delight.

— *William Blake*

A friend gave me an inspirational quotation on a lovely card with hand-painted marbleized triangles in strokes of purple, blue, pink, and various greens. It came in the mail the day before we left with a note that read, "Dear Sandie: Someone sent me this—it might be useful for marginalia?"

> Share your experience. The more selfless you are, the more the self benefits.
>
> —D. MING-DAO

Because the card was so pretty, I had attached it to a binder with a paper clip and brought it with us.

Peter emerged from the dressing area in a pink cotton bathing suit with a coral and blue fish pattern, purchased at the Coco Shop in Antigua the year after we were married. It's beautifully faded from the sun, and sensuously soft. I gave him a few love pats and we were off for a swim before lunch. Peter is a Pisces and loves the beach and water. When he was three, his family lived in Babylon, Long Island, where there was a swimming club on the bay. His mother would swim out to the end of the diving board, and little Peter would be bribed to jump from the wooden board with the promise of a chocolate ice-cream cone. Her outstretched arms encouraged him along with the reward of a sweet. He can still recall how scared he was. He would jump, and once he realized he had survived, he found it all so thrilling. His father had an Elko boat, and they used to take spins to a beach on nearby Fire Island. There were no houses in sight on Fire Island in 1925, and the island was usually deserted except for a few picnickers. He remembers the smell of burning wood from barbecues and the roar of the ocean.

It is only with the heart that one can see rightly; what is essential is invisible to the eye.

—*Antoine de Saint Exupéry*

When Peter's head emerges from the luminous turquoise, his silver hair glistens and I see that unbelievably happy smile. I love playing in the water with Peter. I attach myself to his chest, lock my arms around his neck, and wrap my legs tightly around his waist. He bounces me up and down, then tosses me back into the water. I splash, kick, and dive down to the sandy bottom to do handstands. Below, I feel thousands of circles of pulsating light and energy. In warmth of the air and water, I feel the sun as a living presence. Our swim is totally refreshing, invigorating our bodies, piquing our appetites. The water temperature, an ideal seventy-six degrees, creates a magical first swim that took place within a few yards of where we held hands and ran into the crystal-clear seafoam water nearly twenty-three years ago. How much deeper and richer our love for each other is now, after years of getting to know each other better, of growing and living in love. I feel a distinct newness, as if this were our very first time in the water. As we mature, we experience so many things. We feel blessedness for our ability to participate, to engage fully, in all times, especially those when we focus on each other's love. Peter tenderly wipes my face dry with a huge coral-colored terrycloth towel. I wrap it around my waist for our walk down the beach, tying my sarong around my shoulders so I won't burn. I look over at Peter and marvel at how deep and rich our love for each other is now after so many years. I feel so fortunate to be here, present to life, and living in love with such a man. How can I be so lucky?

Everything appears so natural, so lush. The hibiscus are intense reds, purples, yellows, pinks, and combinations of yellow with pink centers, white with red, all open, vibrant, and verdant, within arm's reach of our table. I will never get used to seeing the fuchsia bougainvillea rising against the whitewashed roofs silhouetted against this ink-stained turquoise sea. Breathing this refreshing ocean air, listening to the pounding surf, feeling the warmth of the sunlight, washed in the colorful wonders of natural beauty will always hit me in the solar plexus. I feel a transmutation where the exchange of energy is circulating love. Can other human beings transform our energy, transcend our perspective into purer spirit, light, and love? Is it possible to empower *ourselves* with an energy of consciousness that has reference points that flow toward wholeness, connec-

> *These are the golden days.*
>
> —*Peter Megargee Brown*

tions, balance and joy? Can our soul be happily at home in our body? Can our medium of expression be one of beauty? Are there visionaries in our midst who help us point upward toward our true, pure nature, helping us shed any artificial facades? Are we able to direct the energy of our soul, no matter what problems we face, remaining loving and whole, integrated human beings? I am dazzled by the moment, entranced, sensuously absorbing the vibrations. I am temporarily linked to divine inspiration, free, in awe, awakening with a quickening of creative impulses, breathing in new life-refreshing energy. I'm moved, tantalized by the stimulation. Is living in love a high aesthetic achievement? Can we preserve within the sanctuary of our own heart an inexhaustible, boundless series of reveries?

Rejoice with me.

—*Luke 15: 6–7*

The American artist and teacher Robert Henri taught us: "We will be happy if we can get around to the idea that art is not an outside and extra thing; that it is a natural outcome of a state of being; that the state of being is the important thing; that a man can be a carpenter and be a great man." How can I maintain this "state of being"? I love Peter and I love the sun, the water, the lobster, and the wine. Beauty makes us feel good and therefore we are more loving. We're able to stand at heights where vulgarity can't exist. Beauty utters our innermost hopes, expresses our faith, answers our dreams. We experience harmony in our senses, through our body. When we're able to fling this essence of purity and happiness into the realm of the intangible, the workings of our spirit, love follows. Beauty's divine attributes inform us what is beautiful is right; it delights to the benefit of all; to the detriment of none.

Grow old along with me!
The best is yet to be,
The last of life, for which the first was made.

—*Robert Browning*

Beauty and love elevate our mood. The electrifying experience of life is here. Who couldn't feel enraptured on an August day in Bermuda when you're on a honeymoon, having achieved a paradigm of living in love? I'm under a spell, and wonder, *Who is the enchanter? What is this aura of romance and love?*

I know Bermuda will be here a long time. In five days I will not be here; someone else will sit in my place. Will it be as beautiful in *their* mind's eye? Few of us live permanently on an island of such beauty. Is happiness possible to maintain? Is it reasonable to feel this sense of appreciation for excellence in the common moments of our daily lives? Was I in a state of readiness, wishing to celebrate life, and spend several unencumbered days with Peter, alone, together, in love? Aristotle encourages us to "trust thyself," understanding a person becomes "self" in relation to another person. Peter expects only that I be myself.

Skill makes love unending.

—Ovid

Essentially, all divine energy flows through each individual human soul. We are the channels, the conduits to bring out what is within. Our biological inheritance, in combination with our environmental influences, are strong factors in our personality. Living involves a continuous way, a process of growth and change. The prime minister of France from 1918 to 1919, George Clemenceau, also known as "the tiger," was a friend of Claude Monet. "Your error," Monet once said to Clemenceau, "is to wish to reduce the world to your measure, whereas, by enlarging your knowledge of things, you will find your knowledge of self enlarged." Our paths are uncharted because they are our own.

Love in the past is only a memory. Love in the future is a fantasy. Only here and now can we truly love.

—Buddha

Peter believes, "When in love, everything is loved. Love blossoms all around." This path is paved with love of every kind imaginable. Above all, *Peter loves.* If we can find ways to direct our energy in loving ways, flinging it out into space, not necessarily toward one person, but through the example of being in love with life, our energy will have a positive effect on those around us.

Loving Living in Color

Of the millions of colors existing in the world, only thousands have been named. I love to identify colors; they whet my appetite for life. I give colors the names of foods and all the wonders of nature. I still can't believe the awesome experience of actually eating colors as beautiful as cantaloupe, papaya, nectarine, peach, apricot, mango, and kumquat. Is there anything more refreshing than the color of a lemon peel?

The bougainvillea that climbs the walls of our cottage is now a blaze of hot pinks, melon shades, and yellows. The variegated green foliage of palm trees and bay grapes are a study in contrast with the plumbago blue sky and the deep delphinium blue of the horizon.

I have seen too much not to be content with my lot.

—*Brooke Astor*

I feel love circulating all around and flowing inside of me. I feel myself lifted into pure spirit, light, and love. I feel empowered by living itself. I feel my soul happy in my body— my body the ideal bridge between this world and the mysterious, spiritual world beyond.

Dancing in the Dark

The evening of our second glorious day in Bermuda was the night of our first dance. This event held a special promise of romance. As we dressed I was reminded of Baudelaire's essay, "In Praise of Cosmetics," where he described our "external finery" as "one of the signs of the primitive nobility of the human soul." I love the way Peter dresses, especially when we're on an island escape, liberated from dark, conservative colors. For our dancing celebration he wore crisp white pants, a double-breasted blue blazer, a red tie with blue tulips, a blue and red silk scarf, and pink socks. Only a really happy, self-assured man wears pink socks.

My newly styled balloon dress feels sassy as I tie a shocking hot fuchsia, quilted silk cummerbund around my waist, putting on some gaudy gold earrings, encrusted with pink, purple, and red stones. I'm a bride again. The dinner date has begun. Off we go to our beloved Fourways restaurant for dining and music.

May you live *all the days of your life.*

—*Jonathan Swift*

Looking across the table at Peter, clinking our glasses: "Cheers." "To us." "To us, darling." I savored the first sip of red Burgundy, enjoying the subtle, velvety bouquet that exuded hints of violets and raspberries. A waiter came to our table offering us hors d'oeuvres. Simultaneously, we both reached to the center, picking sprigs of parsley. I started to giggle, having a sudden recollection of this same sequence that I've shared with Peter since 1956, when Peter's sister had just built a terrace off her living room. I can remember vividly what I said to Peter that evening forty-one years ago. "I never eat standing up," I told him as I nibbled on the parsley. "I don't either," he responded, nibbling on his. I winked and he flashed that radiant smile. Now, wherever we are, whenever we're passed food, we reach for the parsley, a code ritual of our friendship. We've done this thousands of times, and it always has a secret way of gathering all the past memories into the moment.

For one human being to love another: that is perhaps the most difficult of all our tasks, the ultimate, the last test and proof, the work for which all other work is but preparation.

—Rainer Maria Rilke

The restaurant's owner, Mrs. La Farge, comes over to have a visit. Sergio smiles up at us from the piano. I smelled the sizzle of garlic butter at the next table. So many memories of this restaurant strung together over all these years add to my rapture being here with my boyfriend in lively courtship. Love is felt, not spoken. Eating is such a sensual experience, Peter and I make a habit of dining, keeping the flame of love burning. We always dress for dinner, even if this means only changing our shirt or scarf or tie. We freshen up, play music, light candles, and treat our dinner as a date every night, regardless of where we are or if we have friends or family with us. It's at the table, over food, where we review the events of the day, laugh, toast, and discuss our dreams and plans for the future. We stay connected, in the intimacy of our love, through this uninterrupted time. We're unavailable to talk on the telephone during our dinner dates. We both look forward to this special privacy. If we go to a dinner party or host one, or if we go to a restaurant with family or friends, invariably we'll sit alone afterward to listen, to be, to love. After more than eight thousand dinner dates with Peter, our courtship still enlarges us immeasurably.

When we travel, we almost always are together because we treasure our dinner dates. I've been to Montreal as his companion, with no official agenda but the dinner date. While this may not always be economical or efficient, we've made a commitment to our living in love and our eternal honeymoon. When I sacrificed many out-of-town design projects after we were married, I realize now it wasn't just so I could be at the dinner table for the girls, it was also for Peter and me. Going steady, having dinner dates, is far from practical, but we're a pair, and we like the feeling of living in love.

The richest gifts we can bestow are the least marketable.

—*Henry David Thoreau*

The feast begins. Our asparagus is deliciously fresh. The salad of plump, red-red tomatoes and sweet, mild Bermuda onions with the most wonderful creamy vinaigrette dressing awakens new sensations, bringing us pleasure as we feel our bodies being nourished in tandem with our souls. I take time to celebrate, in a moment of blessing, this wonderful food. Eating is so routine to all of us; at the same time it can be an epiphany, every time. How I love to eat. Everything about the ritual is so important to me, opening up all my senses, creating a symphony. Peter and I are careful never to rush each other. There is a sacredness to the moment where timing is everything. Dining on Little Neck clams, savoring their texture, squeezing extra lemon juice on them, adding a touch of fresh horseradish is a sensual experience that should not be hurried. Relishing the smells, the presentation, and the conversation as

Oh, yes, I remember it well.

—*Alan Jay Lerner*

we continue our feast of grilled sole with the freshest of mixed vegetables, listening to lovely melodies of Gershwin, it is easy to love. And imagine, after our dinner date, skipping off to dance under the glitter of an August moon, under the stars. Who could ask for anything more?

On the terrace floor with my balloon skirt swirling in puffy waves around my knees, I feel I'm literally being swept off my feet. Peter wears magically romantic black patent leather shoes whenever we go dancing. As we glide across the terrace floor, sharing glances, holding on with one hand, Peter twirls me away, as if letting me free. We whirl. I dip. Peter pulls me against his chest, showering me with kisses, flirting with me lavishly. I am in ecstasy.

It takes two to tango.

— Proverb

I think about the Broadway musical *Crazy for You*, that foot-thumping, clap-happy tempo of energy where everyone in the audience was full of cheer, and vicariously light as air, living in love. One of the lines from the song "Let's Glorify Love" keeps coming to mind, and "Embraceable You." Peter is my favorite dancing partner. When I'm dancing with him I melt into his rhythm, follow his lead, and am enthralled throughout. I love the way Peter dances, and have never felt awkward or clumsy when we dance even when I trip over him or mess up his lead. I'm entranced by his love of movement. Rhythm and sound are primal and we respond naturally. We feel invigorated when we dance. Dancing unleashes psychic energy, like fireworks on the Fourth of July. When we marry, we dance. When we go on a honeymoon we dance. When we receive good news, we dance. We

Without good eating and drinking love grows cold.

— Terence

skip, jump for joy, and just want to keep moving our feet, letting the beat draw us nearer to each other, and closer to eternity. We dance our hearts out in the glory of love.

Years ago, on a Friday afternoon, I said good-bye to a friend. "Have a great weekend. Sit by the fire and be cozy." "I'm going dancing," my friend replied with a twinkle. You should have seen the expression on her face. We all love to go dancing. In *The New York Times Magazine* in 1995 there was an article entitled "Better than Sex," about Ginger Rogers, who had recently died. "Ginger Rogers has been enshrined in our memories as Fred Astaire's partner. A kind of spontaneous combustion took place when they danced together; they enhanced each other, as all good couples do. . . . The rapid-fire exchanges, the tenderness, the playfulness, the mutual respect, the shared delight—Fred and Ginger's union transcended the mechanics of intercourse." Well said.

When you do dance, I wish you
A wave o' the sea, that you might ever do
Nothing but that.

—William Shakespeare

Other than a few candles placed around the terrace, there is nothing lighting this scene but the glimmer of the moon and the stars. I twirl in circles in the sweet jasmine air. Dancing in my dress with the balloon skirt swirling against the terrace floor, being literally swept off my feet, year after year, I believe I am Peter's Ginger, and I know he is my Fred. We are better dancers now than ever before; we can anticipate each other's moves with more grace. We've been through so much together. Everyone in life is subject to turmoil, challenges, setbacks, failures, illness, and unexpected deaths, but the more we live together in love, the greater our gratitude for the sheer grandeur of life. I feel more alive, more feminine than ever before. I've been here before, but somehow this is all new.

When we return to our cottage, as I open the gate to our private terrace, I see it anew—this incredible place where we have lived so many lives. I have a photograph of my parents taken on their honeymoon, standing on this—was it the very same terrace? How many lovers have been held in its timeless embrace? I try to see the face in the moon but my heart can't stop dancing. So, quietly, after the musicians left, we continue to twirl to the tune of loving energy. "I need someone to watch over me . . . the way you hold your knife . . . the way you dance till three . . . They can't take that away from me . . . He carries the key." Music brings out our feelings, our vibrancy, our spirit. I think of John Lennon's words: "Every day in every way it gets better." Peter is the music of my life.

> *Dancing concerns the body, and music aims at goodness of soul.*
>
> —*Plato*

Our elevated view of each other is a good meeting place where love can thrive. Peter knows my struggles and I know his, and we learn from our challenges and grow in our respect for each other. The eternal honeymoon is alive, and grows more powerful in time. As we walk through the door of our cottage I hum "Some Enchanted Evening." I slip out of my balloon dress and slide between the sheets. Lying there, caressed by the sound of the waves rolling, tumbling to the shore, I give into that wonderful feeling of peaceful bliss at the end of a happy day; I am entranced. Who *could* ask for anything more? Smiling, we drift into divine exultation.

> *It's quite right what they say: the three most beautiful sights in the world are a ship in full sail, a galloping horse, and a woman dancing.*
>
> —*Honoré de Balzac*

Morning Renewal

I never close the curtains when we go to sleep in the cottage in Bermuda because we love waking up naturally to the sunlight. Breakfast is served at eight o'clock on our terrace. We put on our huge bright-white terrycloth robes and pad, barefoot, out to breakfast. "Did you have sweet dreams?" Peter asks. We kiss and I nibble on a sweet berry muffin as I sip fresh orange juice and enjoy a cup of coffee. Our ritual is to remain on the terrace after breakfast, reading and writing until midday. At noon, we go for a cool refreshing swim and spend some time on the beach reading and talking before lunch.

When I return to the terrace, after disappearing into the room to look for our sunglasses, Peter hands me a mint green Bristol card. He stands behind me, rubbing my shoulders and neck as I read his note:

Friday morning

Dear Alexandra,

Here we are together in love, living the moment in joy and serenity. We woke naturally to blue sky, shining sun, and views of the ocean, through windows ringed with morning glory. While you were gone, sugar birds arrived to taste the raspberry muffins and honey. I contemplate the sweet day stretching out ahead of us as a gift. You consume my thoughts and our souls merge as one. You are my love in this heavenly place.

May our love grow and continue forever.

Peter

Before he sits down to continue his breakfast, Peter walks to the edge of the terrace, plucks a pink hibiscus, and brings it over to put into my hair. He takes another bite of his honey-soaked muffin. I answer, "I did have sweet dreams. I relived all the joy of yesterday and last night. It doesn't get much sweeter than this."

Here on this terrace lingering over coffee, I daydream about our lifetime of love together. I think about all we have been through, how much I'm looking forward to the surprises of the future. I think about love, how it peaks when it has time to ripen. I had brought William James's essays to our terrace table that morning and as I begin to read them I nod *yes:* "Be not afraid of life. Believe that life *is* worth living, and your belief will help create the fact." Living in love is up to each of us. Life is what we want it to become, for ourselves and loved ones.

Also on the terrace table is Nikos Kazantzakis's *Report to Greco.* The first time I read this, his final book and report on his life, I was on a family odyssey in Greece in 1976. His major character and friend was Zorba the Greek, one of my favorite souls in literature because of his passion for life. He dared to be free, to be himself, to find happiness in the moment, wherever and whatever he did. On his deathbed he said he had no regrets. Zorba and Kazantzakis were friends, and when Alexis Zorba died, a vision came over Kazantzakis to write a book about him.

I got rhythm, I got music.

—*Ira Gershwin*

I was meant to read this book again on this journey of renewal and discovery. Bermuda and Greece intertwine in my heart because of the light and beauty. Kazantzakis wrote excitedly about the seeds of the myth of Zorba crystallizing in his soul after he received word of Zorba's death. "I do not believe in coincidence," he wrote, "I believe in destiny." (Perhaps Peter's and my union was predetermined, an inevitable fate.) Zorba told Kazantzakis, "I always act as though I were immortal."

Kazantzakis cried out in anger after Alexis Zorba's death, "Unjust! Unjust! Such souls should not die. Will earth, water, fire, and chance ever be able to fashion a Zorba again? . . . I believe him to be immortal . . . How can a fountain like that ever run dry?" The great gift Zorba gave us is this immortality, so we can all know at least one person who knew

I got the sun in the morning and the moon at night.

—Irving Berlin

great joy in living, singing, laughing, dancing, splashing water from the sea into Kazantzakis's face, cleansing him into waking up to the magic of each moment. Zorba even wore a bell so that when he moved around or danced, it rang out. He delighted when people laughed at him because at least they were smiling. He was free, always himself, living in love.

Let your life lightly dance on the edges of Time like dew on the tip of a leaf.

—Rabindranath Tagore

If you know Zorba, you know Peter. Peter has Zorba's spirit. He clicks his fingers and taps his shoes. He shoots the waves and splashes me with water. He whistles, makes bird calls, dances for joy, skips upstairs, singing "Hey, ho." He doesn't need anything to be happy about, he's so filled with gratitude to be living in love. What a transcendent, efflorescent blessing to live in love with such a vital spirit. Peter's energy overflows and refreshes all of us who know and love him. The world is his to explore and love.

But the real gem I rediscovered on the terrace that heavenly morning was reading the tender words of Kazantzakis's wife, Helen. In an introduction to *Report to Greco* she wrote following the author's death: "In my thirty-three years by his

[Kazantzakis's] side I cannot recall ever being ashamed by a single bad action on his part. He was honest, without guile, innocent, infinitely sweet toward others, fierce only toward himself. If he withdrew into solitude, it was only because he felt the labors required of him were severe and his hours numbered."

Her one word for her husband's entire life is "dignity." Nikos Kazantzakis's life in her view was full of substance, of human joy, and pain. She believed, "It was precisely these difficult moments which always served Kazantzakis as new steps enabling him to ascend higher—to ascend and reach the summit he promised himself he would climb before abandoning the tools of labor because night had begun to fall."

To write a good love letter, you ought to begin without knowing what you mean to say, and to finish without knowing what you have written.

—*Jean-Jacques Rousseau*

Peter *is* Zorba; he is also Nikos Kazantzakis, creator of the Zorba character. His passionate love of life is overflowing, rooted in his seriousness, his dedication to excellence, his quest for truth. The reality of Peter's essential personality and integrity frees him to be playful, fun-loving—to kick up his heels in the maturity of life.

The indirect gesture is double.

—*Peter Megargee Brown*

At four o'clock, still impassioned to be together, Peter and I leave the terrace for our afternoon at the beach. We pack some books to take with us. I always carry a tote bag with reading selections and writing materials even though we sometimes stretch out on lounge chairs under an umbrella, falling asleep tranquilized by the rhythms of the waves. On our first honeymoon nearly twenty-three years ago, I carried a tote bag of books, school-girl style, to Paris and then on to Bermuda to Morning Glory Cottage by the sea.

I love the cadence of our days, on vacation as well as at home. We pursue our interests no matter where we find ourselves. At this moment I feel a divine sense of grace. I don't want to fall asleep right away. I want to muse, wondering about expansive visions and thoughts.

> *A pair of star-crossed lovers.*
>
> — *William Shakespeare*

As I drift into the arms of Morpheus I think about our joyful morning and our lovely lunch. I must have French blood, because as soon as I finished lunch, I fantasized about another sumptuous dinner. "Tonight I think I'll have grilled scampi."

Not much reading was done on the beach that afternoon. We stretched out side by side, held hands, as though we were bound at the hip, our breathing synchronized. I love holding Peter's hand. This physical connection merges our souls and I feel strengthened, utterly at peace.

> *I did this, that, and the other thing in my life, yet I did very little.*
>
> — *Zorba the Greek*

I get up to go for a stroll on the beach. Peter follows me. We walk, arm in arm, to the end of the cove before returning to our strip of beach, where we run into the water for a refreshing swim, lots of splashing, and shooting the waves. There's that electric grin again, the one Peter flashes, the one I've grown more and more certain is only meant for me.

How powerful was this eternal honeymoon. We felt lifted up on angel's wings. We enjoyed our walks in gardens, the tranquility of sipping iced tea on quiet verandahs, the temptations of all the fresh fish, vegetables, and fruits. We collected sea shells, watched the island transformed by the warm glow of a setting sun. We reveled in crystal sun by day and danced through starlit evenings, breathing sultry, calm air that intoxicates the spirit. The colors are so delicious, we want to lick them, stain our retina with them, pierce the center of our hearts with them.

Living in love is the experience of oneness.

I want to bottle this honeymoon, capture it, and take it home with me. Short of doing that I put some coral sand into a small plastic bag to bring home. I'll put it in a clear glass dish on my desk in my Zen room. I pack a few shells in a small, blue marbleized box. One suitcase carries all the clothes for the laundry, still carrying the scent and sand of all those hours of enjoyment lived in love.

Returning Home

It's time to go home. But I don't feel any regrets. I feel triumphant. This honeymoon showed me how close we are, how passionately we care about each other, in a tenderness that sweetens the atmosphere wherever we are. We know how to be together living in love better than ever before. We also know what awaits us in our own cottage in Stonington. At home we find visible signs of our accumulated love. We are surrounded by all the paintings and objects we've collected from our loving encounters. We see the things that define us, speak of our sensibility, our love of beauty, and our

Love is all new, fresh.

—Roberto Sció

relationship to others. Here, at home, everything tells a story about our lives. Our honeymoon continues. There, we'll enjoy the same sun, the same sky, the same moon, and the same stars. The same two people will continue to live in love together, wherever we are.

Peter and I are living our love story together, each day. As long as we continue to grow together, to nurture each other's spiritual self, the honeymoon will never end. At home, or wherever our adventure takes us, our honeymoon will go on.

We can all renew our vows to live in love, actively releasing our powers to others. A marriage certificate is no guarantee of a higher state of loving energy. I love Peter with the same love I feel for living. We can all continuously strengthen our

> *Two are better than one.*
>
> —*Ecclesiastes 4:9*

love of life, giving of our true spirit to others, understanding love is always released from within. When we care for others, loving energy increases inexhaustibly.

I could never have known that Peter and I would be living so passionately in love after almost twenty-three years of marriage, growing more in love each day. How could I have known? Until we have felt responsible for the support and nurturing of another soul that is deeply enmeshed with our own, we cannot know the full life-expanding power of love. Until we have learned what it means to give of ourselves,

> *Look homeward, angel!*
>
> —*John Milton*

unselfishly, to compromise for the sake of the well-being of something larger than ourselves, we don't know the triumph of creating happiness in this divine energy. Without others to love we miss an essential creative connection to life. Love has the power to build worlds, to heal, to sustain life—even after death. Love is infinite, divine, eternal. Through our love, we unleash the most powerful force in the universe.

The more time we spend together, the more masterful we become at the art of pleasing each other. When Peter is reading in a comfortable chair with his feet up, I don't suggest he put out the recycling. We're able to work things out fully in our minds because we've shared so many experiences, been through so much together. We've had time to consider various ways to ripen the fruits of our lives so there is greater flavor and sweetness. We move ourselves into a desired framework. All the growth, the intellectual illumination, the ripening of the personality allows us to embrace change because this amplifies love. There's a greater buoyancy, an ability to recover quickly from setbacks when you have more accumulated, mutual experiences.

First there was today, and then it would be tomorrow, but beyond that things like next week were quite remote.

—*Eva Figes*

Through all these years you become increasingly stimulated intellectually and aesthetically, appreciating refinement and style. You absorb this intangible development of personality and in this maturing process there is greater understanding. Throughout all the life chapters, living has learning qualities that accumulatively make a great difference to your ability to live in a loving consciousness.

I want to do with you What the spring does With the cherry trees.

—*Pablo Neruda*

The essence of one's love, flowing as a river, never arriving at total knowledge or being able to understand the mystery, we grow up the way a tree does, with many branches that flower and bear fruit. We have more to appreciate, we've triumphed over so much, had little epiphanies along the path, growing more patient, more tolerant, growing closer, over time.

The surprises of joy accumulate when granddaughter Julia, on our return from Bermuda, introduces us to her fourth-grade English class, "This is my grandma. This is my grandpa." These blessings branch out in all directions, and are at the root of our luminous souls. We awaken anew each day to this richness, this extreme happiness, receiving pleasure from a wink, an ecstatic glance, or that smile that has wings. When there is kaleidoscope range, this expansive frame of reference, there is a feeling of equilibrium, of contentment, of everlasting love and light.

*Love only is eternal,
Love only does
not die.*

—*Harry Kemp*

If there is any way for one human being to transcend the limits of death and darkness, in hopes of the glory of living immortally in the light, it is to live in love.

Ways to Live in Love

We weave golden threads of love by tapping into our inner resources, connecting with the universal flow of energy that is love. Only by releasing this force from within can our spirit be channeled so we become more pure, open, and loving. We are not I-I-I or you-you-you; we meet in the space between us, and here, in this place, the energy can be sublime.

There has recently been a heralded discovery of forty billion more galaxies. To put this into perspective, the sun is only one of fifty to a hundred billion stars in the Milky Way. The potential for further discovery is endless, just as your potential to love has no bounds. In love, you are pure energy, out of time and space; billions of new galaxies are patiently waiting for you to reveal their existence. This magical energy is expansive, inexhaustible, infinite, filled with a divine presence, only requiring you to unfold, giving of your goodness, from your essence.

The dynamics of nature teach us about our human condition and potential, our capacity for transformation. Scientists inform us that 99% of the cells in our body are renewed within one year, just as nature renews itself with each passing season. As our bodies refurbish their cells, we need to refresh and restore the spirit of our nonphysical being so that we become rejuvenated, mind, body, and soul, with pure, vital light.

By closely observing nature, we are refreshed, gaining insights into the limitations of our human nature, connecting with our eternal spirit. No single object stands by itself in this world; everything and every person is connected. When we accept this interconnectedness as truth, we create larger spaces where loving energy can flow. Our relationships with one another can be synergistic, the energy we create when we're together being greater than if we were alone.

We are all spiritual souls, here on earth for a split second of time, to learn about our higher power, our divine, not human, nature. What is most hidden, what is infinite and eternal, is real. The greater our capacity to infuse our selves with loving energy, the stronger our ability will be to bring more light into our lives and the lives of others. By being *present*, being more aware, we feel, as well as see, the bigger picture. We become more whole, more true, and in this way we grow to appreciate an awesome universe from our enlarged perspective.

Our existence is a divine gift. Each of us is capable of contributing more than we could ever imagine to the collective universal loving energy that connects us in a higher place. This openness where our inner resources of love are able to pour out of us effortlessly, spontaneously, freeing us to reach out and touch someone's soul, is ecstasy. We all can affirm life's sanctity and love unconditionally when we understand our potential to live in love. Living in love is an attitude and a way. Over the years I've found certain truths that have been helpful to me and may be helpful to you. I offer them to you, with love. When we both desire the energy between us to be loving, we will be on our path toward divine light, more galaxies, more pure joy.

✳ Commitment

When we entrust our lives to each other for safekeeping, we accept an obligation. Commitment is the keystone of a relationship, the wedge-shaped stone of an arch that locks its parts together in love. When this key element is in place, two people can move far beyond what they're capable of alone.

We make a commitment to our *self* before we commit to each other. Only when we commit to valuing the gift of our own life and do what we can to be and know our *self*, are we capable of making a commitment to another life. Then we can move forward *together* with confidence that we will continue to live and grow in love, secure in the power of the spirit of unqualified love and support for each other.

Trust

How pure the space and energy between us can be when we rely on each other's authenticity, character, truthfulness, and openness. How wonderfully free we feel when we share this mutual trust and confidence. Trust develops and increases over time, but paradoxically, our intuition may be the lodestar that guides reliance on others and ourselves. Trust is the bedrock of love, the glue of all relationships. When this foundation is established, there are no boundaries, only fresh, new adventures of living in love.

Faith

My belief in the beauty and goodness of life on earth, here, now, makes it possible for me to live in love. Faith enables us, without concrete evidence, to maintain a reverence for the spiritual, intangible realities of life and to look inward and upward, catching glimpses of our own divinity. Each of our lives has meaning unique from that of every other individual soul.

Together, we can help each other to seek and find as much illumination as is humanly possible in our brief lifetime. No matter what obstacles we face along the way, they will never grow larger than our divine mission to remain loving, and triumph over natural losses, pain, and sorrows. My faith extends into our relationship with each other. I know we will face detours along our joint path, but we will withstand these hardships, never allowing them to whelm us or conflict with the loving energy between us.

Empathy

When we develop the power to identify ourselves emotionally with another person, and therefore open up to that soul fully, we are living in pure light. This is hard to do, as we are all vulnerable to allowing our own lives, our own autobiographies to interfere with the reality of another human being. To empathize, we must forego our egos (perhaps 90 percent of our nonphysical selves); we must shed the narcissistic side of our nature and mix our hearts one with another.

Empathy derives from the Greek *empatheia,* feeling. We *feel* another person's pain, agony, struggles, lack of confidence, fear of loss; in this brokenness we ourselves grow more human, more real. When we empathize, we connect in the sacred space between us, where we can live in love.

Compassion

When we experience suffering in our own lives, we are more awake to the agony that is a part of the human condition. Because of our own painful experiences, we learn to participate in others' suffering to help alleviate their pain. All of us experience conflict and loss, and our soul hungers for an unobtainable permanence and place in a transient lifetime with an environment in perpetual flux. To show compassion for another human being is to sympathize with them, offering sincere condolence because we have experienced the wounded stripes of pain and anxiety.

We are each compassionate in our own tender, responsive ways, our warmheartedness, cheerful disposition, sensitivity, our sweetness. Positive energy directed toward the healing and enlightenment of another soul is always felt and appreciated because it is genuine. Compassion is grace in action. When we show compassion, we are participating in the loving energy around us; we are living in love.

✳ Understanding

Possessing good judgment, being tolerant, and having a forgiving nature are all faculties of our intuitive emotional intelligence, enabling us to live in love. When confronted with another human soul's predicament, we need to listen to that person and respond with patience and reason; we must be able to absorb information without hasty judgment, without feeling haughty or superior.

When we understand another person's actions or decisions, we do not have to agree with them, but instead, create a harmonious place with room to probe larger dimensions, envisioning clearer insights and resolutions. As we proceed on our path in this understanding state, we appreciate the dynamic nature of the universe and its inhabitants. Everything then seems to come together, toward greater wholeness and harmony.

❉ Communication

Words express our soul. By being aware of our vocabulary, we can express our affections, our appreciations and our exultations, communicating the infallibility of the divine, the sacredness of life, as well as the common, the ordinary. How can we come closer, understand each other better, share more fully in the excellence of our thoughts and emotions? How can we listen more lovingly to the space between us?

In order to live in love together, our personal intercourse must be consistent and genuine, enabling our relationship to grow continuously. We communicate through conversation, exchanging information, ideas, opinions, interests, advice, and feelings, whether they are abstract or concrete. We share our concerns, apprehensions, and troubles as well as our inspiration, good tidings, ecstasy, and rapture. We give and take and elaborate to each other, expressing personal metaphors. As we make ourselves more familiar, we open wide to our spiritual, metaphysical nature, deepening our bond.

But our nonverbal communication can be as important as the spoken word. It is in silence that we're allowed to listen to and hear the inner workings of each other's soul, contemplating our common participation in the space between us. Here we commune through beauty, whether we experience together the exhilarating colors of nature or a symphony of inspirational music. Profound intimacy is felt in shared silence.

When we communicate, we transcend our singleness to our interconnectedness. In open, feeling ways, we increase our awareness of life's possibilities. It is through this communion that we learn about each other and ourselves, deepening our appreciation and awareness of the awesome potential of human relations and love.

❋ Developing Yourself

Within ourselves we have all the wealth we need to live in love. But to do this requires living up to our fullest possibilities and giving birth to our higher power. In order to develop ourselves, as a seed into a plant, as a human being from an embryo, we need to evolve, unfold, bringing out of hiding potentialities solely ours. How can we accomplish what we were put on this earth to do? How can we release our full powers so we're able to use our natural talents? Our individual creativity, our curiosity to learn and grow wiser is an awakening of our higher natures. Our powers to redirect our energies so these gifts are brought out through us are great. The more productive our orientation to life, the more connected we are to our passions, the more joy we experience.

This evolutionary transformation is up to each one of us to discover and pursue. We cannot expect someone else to complete us, to make up for our undeveloped self. No human being can ever find contentment living vicariously through another person. Maturity leads to fulfillment, contentment, and pleasure in the process. Living in love requires direct experience, where we put our *self* to the test of life.

We must believe in our uniqueness, knowing that each of us can do what no one has done before us. We can inspire others when we enjoy our work, not solely the result of our efforts but the moment by moment process of bringing something from inside us out for others to appreciate. For our work to be of interest to others, first we have to be interested in what we're doing, and do it for the sheer sake of our own pleasure and fulfillment. If I am bored, I will bore you. If I'm inspired, there is a chance you will connect to my energy. Everything we do to develop our sensitive nature is good for us and consequently good for others. All we imagine and appreciate as beautiful can be wise and wonderful, worthy of our passionate attention. We should cherish our interests, whatever they are, and delight in exposing them to others.

We never reach a place where we feel we've arrived, where we can rest on our laurels, because the joy is in the activity, in honing our crafts continuously and in discovering new involvements of importance, in the flow of work. If, through the process as well as the results of work or creation, we try to make sense out of the world, each of us can add to this collective pool of consciousness. We express our vision of the world through what gifts we bring out of us. Here the invisible love is made visible because of our efforts, our discipline, and actions.

Love is an energy that requires exercising. Whatever time and effort it takes for you to develop your *self* so you are a more loving, giving person, more aware of your own gifts and talents, more generous to yourself to nourish and nurture them, the more you will live in loving energy. And the more you develop your *self,* the more free you are to enable others to express the loving energy in themselves. The space between you is elevated because the goodness in your heart is expressed. Creative self-expression is at the core of living in love because it is blessed by divine inspiration, your higher power.

❉ Encouragement

We all have unique, individual talents, but that doesn't mean they will flow automatically from our inside out. We tap into the loving energy of others to help inspire us along our path of personal development. We cherish their encouragement, knowing how vital the assistance of others is to our well-being.

Whenever we help someone dare to do what is difficult, we fill them with courage and strength of purpose. I want to be an encourager, fostering, promoting, recommending, and giving cheer to help someone to do what is in them to accomplish. When our intentions are to help raise confidence and hope, we strengthen and stimulate the other person to wise action.

Encouragement is a selfless contribution, and, when we live in love, one of the essential ways we show our affection. All the heroic geniuses of the past, who encourage us by their legacy, were themselves encouraged by loving teachers and mentors. Be an illuminator to those around you. The space between you and the people you encourage is intensely loving. Think of all the people who have spread light on your path and bless them with appreciation.

Mutuality

When we share our passions, we magnify each other's energy. We respond to the richness of life together. How can we better relate to each other as we progress on our path so this loving force will build? How can we commingle, blending together spiritually?

We need some common ground to live and to grow in love with another person. True opposites, despite much myth, do not attract for the long term. Mutuality requires some compatibility in temperament, energy, and spirit as well as a frame of reference. It is wise to spend our "between us" time with people who are committed to the pursuit of knowledge, the appreciation of beauty, and making a contribution leading to a happier life.

Reciprocity, a key component of mutuality, is a universal energy where we give our spark to others and they to us. This exchange is love in action, living in love, right where we are. Nothing is one sided. I respond to you and you to me; together we look up higher than any height we could reach on our own. We know the song of each other's heart, and together we sing our own duet, easing our pain and intensifying our joy.

✳ Transference of Energy

Your life is continuously influenced by the energy of others. How can we redirect and maintain our energy flow to inspire, and not damage, the karma of our human environment? How can we maintain a consistent, positive transference of energy throughout our life?

Positive energy builds only on its own momentum. The more energy you expend in a loving conscience, the more loving energy you will generate outward, revitalizing your sensibilities in all areas of your life. Always remember that love is inexhaustible. When we do not use our energy in loving ways, releasing negative energy, we become our own nemesis. The difference between happiness and madness depends on how we discharge our energy. Are we intoxicated by the sheer joy of living and loving, spreading this ecstasy to others, or are we depressed, anxious, and unhappy? All of us have egos that need harnessing, biological genes to contend with, temperaments and histories to put in perspective, but we can work harder to let the light shine through us.

Love is the core of human existence. Therefore we need to increase our capacity to love on earth the human beings we come into contact with every day, never blocking our channels or withholding love from one another. Loving energy is not meant to be conserved, but to be used generously throughout our lives. Efficiency plays little part in the transference of energy between human souls. Machines are efficient, cold in their absence of humanity and intuition, eventually obsolete when newer models arrive. You can't have faith in a machine because it *cannot* love you. Loving energy on the other hand is timeless, out of space, perpetuating, continuous, available to all who seek its wonder. I don't have to be with you to love you.

How do you want to discharge your energy? How much of your life is involved with others in interaction of caring and loving? How do you treat the people in your daily life? How do you assess your capacity to love? How do you want to live your life?

The resources we can draw on to help channel our energy toward goodness and love can be boundless. When we're able to transfer our energy in love, the space between us is invigorated and refreshingly pure.

❇ Positive Attitude

Our attitude toward the way we approach our daily lives plays an integral role in our capacity to live in love. To have a positive attitude, concentrating our minds on the good and constructive aspects of life, is elemental to embracing all the gifts life has to offer. What is your attitude? What do you consider to be your basic disposition? Do you believe your thinking and behavior is reasonable, objective and fair, without prejudice? Do you believe you can change your predilections, leaning more toward what is true, good, and honest?

Our outlook should always be on the path of light, away from darkness. A negative attitude, one that is indifferent or harmful, hollow or muddled, dissipates energy, darkens and pushes away from those around us. When we focus positively and affectionately, our actions will enhance the vital energy coming from within ourselves. Think of yourself as a force of positive electric charges directing your energy in ways that increase your potential. You will find you can also give positive contributions, helping solve problems, finding solutions.

Weathering life's storms and complexities without becoming cynical and bitter is one of life's greatest challenges. Mental flexibility is necessary in order to maintain an optimistic attitude toward life, especially in times of adversity. We must keep in mind that we are a myriad mix of polar opposites, and, in our polarity, we become more positive only when we are less negative. Staying on a path of light may at times require a deliberate effort, but inevitably it will bring about desired responses. Through regular meditation, being outside in nature's beauty, seeking the company of spiritually developed people, reading good literature, retreating into solitude when you need to hear your inner callings, you can maintain a loving consciousness.

A positive attitude is a gift you can give to yourself, and a blessing to those around you.

�֎ Responsibility

Answering for our actions and decisions and fulfilling our own basic needs and obligations are vital to any foundation of happiness and living in love. If we do not have a solid sense of personal responsibility, we are denying ourselves a full life, and we will be a burden to those around us.

We cannot have a genuine relationship if we ignore personal responsibility, because if we are not accountable for ourselves, we cannot make a genuine commitment to others. How can we be reliable when we expect others to take care of us? How can

we earn another's trust in us, if we have not learned how to fulfill, as best we can, our own needs and obligations?

Our own happiness is no one else's responsibility but our
own. If each of us took charge of our own life and found a variety of outlets for our own soothing and pleasure, then the
"between-us" space more likely would be charged with fresh
vitality and enthusiasm. But when one person is irresponsible,
defensive, unfairly blaming others for their own emptiness, that
person's neediness and immaturity can depreciate the well-
being of others.

Maturity requires that we no longer hold others accountable
for our actions and decisions, and that we never set unrealistic
expectations centered on what others should do for us. Only
then will we be free to give of ourselves in a genuine light.
When we live by a discipline of personal responsibility, we have
cleared the path for genuine loving relationships.

❋ Respect

If the energy of love is to flow from us to others in constructive, giving ways, our hearts must first be full of this energy
before we can channel it. The same theory applies to respect.
Only when we have self-respect, will we appreciate, respect,
and esteem others.

Respect requires a conscious consideration for other people's feelings. I may not agree with you, but I respect your feelings and views. We cannot force our opinions on each other, but
we can respect our differences. Doing this helps us to evolve
into kinder human beings.

Are all people worthy of our respect? Do all people have
credibility? There will always be certain individuals we feel par-

tiality for due to what we think are their developed souls and intelligence. We admire someone who lives in awareness of their higher power, inspiring our own spiritual development. But to spread our loving energy to all, we must respect the dignity of every human soul.

When we respect everything that is positive and good in each other, and treat our differences with consideration, we may serve as examples, inspiring each other to have a greater reverence for the sanctity of life.

Privacy

To live in love, we all require periods of solitude. To maintain the loving energy within a relationship, we must hold as sacred our time alone, together. Privacy is a gift, a high commitment. I require a large portion of my time to be spent privately, personally, unavailable to intrusion.

Why is it, do you think, people who seek enlightenment escape to a quiet secluded place to meditate? There are times when the most loving thing we can do is to retreat. When we take the time to replenish our inner resources, we bring more light into our relationships with others. Life is a spiritual adventure and should never become superficial. We are who we are because of all our relationships with other human souls, as we engage our higher power in solitude.

When we are silent, we provide a space where we don't hide from our soul. We give our presence to *be*-ing still. There's an awesome mystery in meditation, but the solitude encountered is your *self*. In the deepest depths of your silence there is the truth about you. We learn more about our *selves* when we remain silent than when we're engaged in interaction with others.

Wisdom comes from our presence, more complete in solitude. Here, there is no one to impress, nothing to demonstrate, and nothing to have. We become mindful of ourselves and others.

By being present in silence we can create a state of mind-*full*-ness. The mind acquires soaring space. We see, as if for the first time, a clarity of reality, we experience what is there, what is essentially *us*. We begin to hear music, and we let our silence sing.

Lack of personal space causes stress and strain and therefore is dangerous to our health. We should relish our solitude, and seize it especially when we feel a need to reawaken our senses and spirit. How do you know when it's time to get away from it all? Whenever you feel discouraged, anxious, or upset, you are off your path; silence is the beam of pure light guiding you back to wholeness.

In loving relationships we need regular periods of solitude *for two* in order to encounter this sacred "between us" space in its authenticity. When we are alone, together, we are fully present for each other; nothing is there to block the loving energy between us. Privacy, for one or for two, is essential, a prerequisite, to living well and growing in love.

❋ Enthusiasm

Mental and spiritual vitality, a zest for living, brings us an abundance of rapture and joy that is contagious. Being an enthusiastic soul opens up fields of opportunity and success, expanding the degree of intensity of our limitless passions, opening wide the boundless wonders of our curiosity.

Enthusiasm is rooted in the Greek word *entheos*, God or God-filled. Enthusiastic people have an exuberance of almost supernatural inspiration, possessing keen and ardent interest in all that life has to offer. When we are enthusiastic, we have a heightened sensitivity toward inspiration, finding it everywhere in everything and everyone.

When we are genuine in our interests, free to *be* ourselves, our spirit benefits from the sincerity we experience, releasing more loving energy. How can we increase and use our enthusiastic nature? What are we passionate about? What astounds us? What are the things we most look forward to? What touches our spirit is of great significance, no matter how simple or complex, and our enthusiasm is how we honor this divine inspiration. Enthusiasm requires humility about all that is available to us, needing a degree of unsophistication. The sheer joy of a new day is cause for genuine excitement. Maintaining a childlike enthusiasm for the common things at hand, right in front of our eyes, our nose, our ears, our mouth is the province of artists. We show our bliss for being alive by increasing our enthusiasms.

Our innate enthusiasm awakens us continuously to all that life has to offer us, in nature, at home, in our relationships, and inside our mind and heart. Once we step into this refreshing reservoir, our enthusiasm is both sincere and infectious, enhancing the loving energy we channel to others.

❀ Mystery

We have to make up our minds now that we will never know enough totally to satisfy our curiosity, or be able to put all the pieces of the puzzle of life together. There's an alchemy even in the puzzle. We must accept that we will never have all the answers before we can live in love. We don't even know all the questions. In jumping into the flow of the mystery, we experience love's divine force. This means acknowledging that we are never fully in control, and there are no guarantees. Life is ultimately a mystery, a series of direct experiences beyond scientific analysis and proof.

To insist we can have all the answers is simplistic. Wisdom acknowledges we will never know; we can only have faith and become informed by our intelligence, our senses, and our intuition. Even when we're intellectually curious, we may be using only 10% of our brain's capacity. Human reason is incapable of solving problems beyond current knowledge and understanding. Our soul is capable of communing through intuition with the divine, of having mystical experiences of unity with the universe. This sacred, peaceful union is the source of spiritual rapture. But we can feel inner peace only when we accept the unknown, the mystery that currently transcends human knowledge.

Just as life is a mystery, so are all of us. Every human being is uniquely gifted, and will be on a different place on their path than we are. We are not riddles to be solved, or here to challenge someone's power to figure us out.

When we try to put an explanation or meaning to everything, we may only subtract from the pure exultation of our experience. We kill a flower when we rip it up from its roots. A child will not open up under constant critical pressure. We experience the flower and the child with a loving heart without surgery or crushing analysis.

Live in the light of pure experience and enjoy the questions, not always demanding answers. We need to relish the mystery, the galaxies, live in the intrigue of moments out of time, out of body, out of space.

❈ Consciousness

When we open our minds to all that is going on around us, when we become more aware and mindful, we come closer to the truth about living in love. When we heighten our consciousness about all our experiences, we become more wise, more in touch with our higher selves and the loving energy that comes from within us and surrounds us.

We need to be conscious in order to avoid unintentionally shutting off any pipelines of loving energy. Be conscious of your priorities. When we lose touch with what's important, when we're not aware, we lose our perspective, causing communication problems, and creating chaos in our lives.

Reaching a high level of consciousness requires time and contemplation; there are no substitutes or shortcuts. First we must get in touch with our higher self, and to do so requires a great deal of discipline and self-knowledge. Once we're capable of emptying our minds so we're able to soak everything in, understanding the depth of our experiences and our feelings, we gain a clearer perspective about ourselves. Our sleep subconsciousness, our dreams, become less abstract, more a part of our wholeness, our integrated self.

As we progress into higher states of consciousness we absorb more, approaching life with an exalted awareness, experiencing life with more intensity, just as a wide-angle lens on a camera has a vaster perspective than a zoom lens that only focuses on a tight detail. We become aware how vulnerable we are to everyone and everything around us, confirming that we are on our path, and here, we have the potential to live in love. Once we reach this level, light, love, and pure energy can flow through us.

Consciousness awakens us to the candle lit in our soul. We all can rise to a higher consciousness, maximizing the loving energy we channel to others, when we live as though we're on borrowed time. If this is our last moment on earth, does this raise our consciousness?

Zen

Once we grasp the truth that there are no absolute answers to being human, we can gain meaning by going with the flow, accepting what's happening as we go along our path. Time is too short to get caught up in trying to change what we have no control over and not to appreciate the sun while it still shines on us. Life has gone on a long time before us and will continue to manage quite nicely without us.

If we're able, in our all too brief time on earth, to create our own personal form of immortality, we need to do it here, now, before it's too late. We should avoid concentrating on trivialities, and focus on the vision of living in love this present moment. Any illumination and enlightenment comes from paying attention to each precious moment as it slips away. All the time we spend rushing or being anxious is wasting our precious resources. We don't have time to rush. Manic hurry is stressful and blocks natural rhythms of contentment and harmony with others.

By living fully in the moment, understanding that the past as well as the future are here in the present, we will enlarge our capacity to love, increase the quality of our longevity, and figure out that heaven is here, now. Living in love is the best vision I have of heaven. Right here, right now, the sun is shining somewhere. If it's storming outside your window, you can remain calm inside your own heart. You have the power to illuminate this moment; that's why we have lamps. That's why we have souls. The light can always be on inside you even when darkness surrounds you.

We need to live in the universal timelessness of love, where what *is* becomes our teacher, where the here and now is all we know, and need to know, of life and living in love.

Grace

We're already at the banquet, enjoying the feast. While the menu changes depending on our circumstances and good fortune, we're alive, *living*. The choice to live in love is ours. Every human being has been given the gift at birth of being touched with a spark of divinity, and with this brief flash of light the potential to live in love is set in motion. When we open up to our innate divinity, we become part of a universal loving energy. This is where we discover grace.

As human beings with divine souls, none of us is ever justified in hurting another person. Our belief in the sacredness of life helps us to replace negative energy felt toward others with compassion, understanding, empathy, and love. This has been confirmed over history by the lives of spiritual guides who teach us about the energy, health, and wisdom of love.

Love me in my brokenness, love me as I am, because we are all here together, and the divine spirit in you is touching this same spirit in me. Grace is the linchpin that holds us together in wholeness and harmony. When we live in love, grace is our bonus. More love and more grace to you, all the days of your life.

I can't give you anything but love . . .

— MOST POPULAR SONG IN
PARIS IN THE 1920s